THE ESSENTIAL
Lake George
BOATERS GUIDE

Fourth Edition

Everything You Should Know
for Fun, Safe and Responsible Boating
on the Queen of American Lakes

Capt. Scott A. Padeni
Peggy Huckel

Quarterdeck Productions

Wilton, New York

www.theessentiallakegeorgeboatersguide.com

Published by:
Quarterdeck Productions.
Wilton CPU Box 2384
Gansevoort, NY 12831
518-587-0734

ISBN: 978-0-692-42511-4

CAUTION: Outdoor recreational activities are by their very nature
potentially hazardous and contain risk. See "Cautions" on next page.

Front cover: Design by Ron Toelke

Front cover photo: View north from the deck of the Horicon docked at
the southwest corner of the lake, photo by Scott Padeni

Back cover photo: View north toward the Canoe Islands, with Tongue
Mountain in the background, photo by Scott A. Padeni

Maps by Scott A. Padeni and Ron Toelke

Publication design and production: Toelke Associates, Chatham, NY
www.toelkeassociates.com

IMPORTANT: CAUTION

This guide is intended as a source of general information only. It is not meant as a replacement for existing nautical charts or other available information regarding boating and other water activities on Lake George or other New York State waterways. Every effort has been made to describe lake conditions accurately. However, the publisher makes no warranty, express or implied, for any omissions or errors in this guide. Boaters should use this guide only as a supplement to the above-mentioned nautical charts and other sources of information, existing aids to navigation, and safe boating practices, and not place undue reliance on its accuracy.

The Essential Lake George Boaters Guide is not intended to be an exclusive source for navigational purposes. All locations and descriptions must be considered approximate. Lake conditions, aids to navigation, lake feature locations and other general lake information were taken from personal observation by the author, as well as from public domain sources including the Lake George Fishing and Boating Map, produced by the Lake George Park Commission and Warren County Tourism Department; NY Lake Contour Maps, produced by the NY State DEC; USGS Topographic maps; "Chart of Lake George" by S. R. Stoddard; and hydrographic data and aerial imagery from the NY State GIS Clearinghouse. *The Essential Lake George Boaters Guide* is a "living document" and we welcome feedback regarding any errors, omissions, corrections, or general suggestions to be incorporated into future editions.

IMPORTANT: CAUTION WHEN USING THE MAPS

The maps prepared for this guide are for informational purposes only, and are not intended to replace existing navigational charts of Lake George. Map locations of all Aids To Navigation (ATONs) and suggested routes are approximate, and should be verified by additional sources and by personal observation while on the water. Every effort has been made to correctly locate ATONs and map routes, but given the scale of the maps and size of the icon graphics, locations cannot be exact. Use caution and common sense when referring to the maps.

Table of Contents

Dedication

I would like to dedicate this fourth edition of *The Essential Lake George Boaters Guide* to all of those individuals and organizations fighting to protect Lake George's natural beauty. As in years past, Lake George is again under siege, though this time it is not marked by the thunder of cannon, but rather by the silent incursion of a myriad of invasive species such as Eurasian Milfoil, Zebra Mussels, Alewives, Water Chestnuts, Spiny and Fishhook Waterfleas, the Asian Clam, and most recently, Chinese Mystery Snails. If left unchecked, these invaders could have a devastating impact on the lake and its water quality, not to mention local businesses whose livelihoods depend so heavily on the lake's beauty. It is my sincere hope that through public awareness, *The Essential Lake George Boaters Guide* can play a small part in protecting the lake, and in Thomas Jefferson's words, its waters "as limpid as crystal."

Capt. Scott A. Padeni

Foreword

Lake George has long been considered a special place by visitors who have marveled at its magnificent scenery and crystal clear waters. Soldiers serving during the French and Indian War and the American Revolution recognized the uniqueness of the setting. In the spring of 1776, Charles Carroll, appointed an emissary to Canada by the Continental Congress, traveled north on Lake George aboard a bateau, noting that he had never seen "water more transparent" with such an abundance of fish. In 1819 Benjaman Silliman, a professor from Yale College, remarked that "every one has heard of the transparency of the water of Lake George," which allowed a fisherman to "select his fish, by bringing the hook near the mouth" even in water 20 to 25 feet deep.

The combination of beautiful scenery along the lake, the history of the region, and the crucial geographical position of the lake between the Hudson River and Lake Champlain helped to develop Lake George as one of the earliest resorts in America. During the nineteenth century the lake became a must-see destination on the grand tour of America. In 1834 Harriet Martineau, a well-known literary figure from England, arrived in America for a tour of the country, noting that of all sites that she wished to visit, Lake George "of all others, I most desired to see," and for the rest of her life her memory was "treated with some flitting image of Lake George."

Scott Padeni's Boaters Guide does justice to Lake George as a premier tourist destination. It provides comprehensive coverage of all aspects of boating on the lake and encompasses the history of the region, points of interest, recreational activities, lodging, etc. It is reminiscent of the celebrated guidebooks of the late nineteenth and early twentieth centuries, including those of Seneca Ray Stoddard. Scott Padeni is an accomplished professional archaeologist, historian, scuba diver, and former captain of the tour boat *Horicon* on Lake George. There is no one more qualified to write a boaters guide to Lake George.

Russell P. Bellico
Author of *Sails and Steam in the Mountains* and
Chronicles of Lake George: Journeys in War and Peace

Introduction

This guide is written for those who enjoy the discovery of tranquil anchorages, breathtaking views, and for those who just love being on the water. Lake George represents one of the most spectacular boating destinations in the country, offering something for everyone: sailing, hiking, kayaking, fishing, scuba diving, and much more. Your Lake George boating experience can be as exciting or as relaxing as you like. Enjoy weekly fireworks, nightclubs, dock and dine restaurants, parasailing, shopping, and jet skiing. Or escape to the solitude of your own private island campsite, where you can watch eagles soar overhead, or hike among the towering Adirondack peaks skirting the lake.

For the history buff, Lake George was the scene of some of North America's most important battles during the French and Indian War and the American Revolution. Today, you can follow in their footsteps with a visit to Fort William Henry, Fort Ticonderoga and numerous other historic sites along the lake. Or experience the lives of the rich and famous as you cruise by their opulent mansions built along Millionaires' Row during the 19th century.

This boating guide is packed with information to help you enjoy everything Lake George has to offer, while staying safe and out of trouble. It provides important boating information on marinas, boat launches, available dockage, anchorages, Lake George regulations, aids to navigation, "rules of the road," and emergency information. With the aid of aerial imagery, shoals and other hazards on the lake are also described in detail. The guide also includes details on lodging, dock-'n-dine restaurants, beaches, attractions, hiking, kayaking and just about everything else you will need to know for an enjoyable time on the lake.

So pull up a seat, open up our guide, and prepare for a great adventure on the "Queen of American Lakes."

Capt. Scott A. Padeni
April 2015

Acknowledgements

No boaters guide could be compiled through the knowledge and experiences of any one individual. I am deeply indebted to the support and assistance of hundreds of Lake George business owners, residents, and boating enthusiasts who provided information, corrections, suggestions and support in this endeavor. I would like to thank Richard and Phyllis Affinito, Vinnie and Louise Barcia, Capt. Paul Boivin, Dan Callahan, Kathy Cifrino, Elaine Chiovarou-Brown (Bolton Chamber of Commerce), Capt. Craig Clesceri, Luisa Craig-Sherman, Richard Conine, Joelle Ernst (Fisheries Biologist, NYS DEC), Amanda Felt, Matt Finley, Captain William Gates, Kevin Griswold, Capt. John Kearney, Capt. Ed Kluck, C. Walter Lender (Executive Director, Lake George Association [LGA]), David McAneny, Joseph Martucci (NYS GIS Clearinghouse, Office of Cyber Security), Ken Parker, Michelle Pollock (LG Kayak Company), Ellen and Dave Pressman, Sally Rypkema, John Scarano (Scarano Boat Building Co.), Gene Tozzi, Chuck Vandrei (NYS DEC), Michelle Way (Lake George Park Commission), Mike White (Executive Director, Lake George Park Commission), John Whitney, and Lori Willard. I am very grateful to Carl Heilman for contributing a selection of beautiful Lake George region photos. Special thanks go to contributors and close friends Russell P. Bellico, Bob Cifrino, Joe DiNapoli, Emily DeBolt (LGA Director of Education), Capt. Bill Dow, Capt. William Gates, Patty Pensel, Jim Quirk, Joseph Zarzynski (Bateaux Below, Inc.) and particularly to Ron Toelke, Barbara Kempler-Toelke, and co-author Peggy Huckel without whose knowledge, assistance, and infinite support this project would not be possible.

And finally, I would like to thank my wife Lori and daughter Melissa for their inspiration and continued support over the years.

The Battle Monument in Lake George State Park depicts the Mohawk chief King Hendrick and British General William Johnson. It stands on the site of the second engagement of the Battle of Lake George (1755). The monument was erected by the Society of Colonial Wars in the State of New York. Photo by Scott Padeni

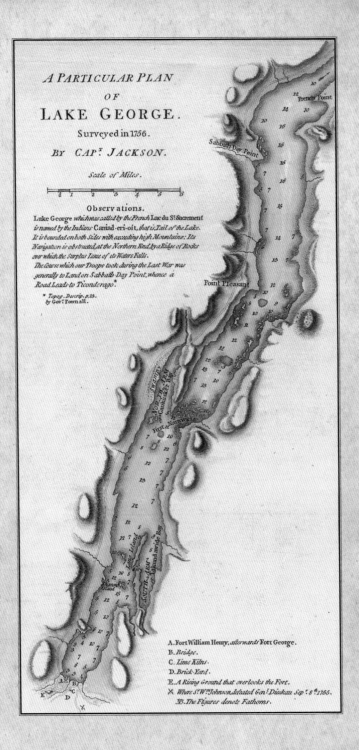

A PARTICULAR PLAN
OF
LAKE GEORGE.
Surveyed in 1756.
By CAPT. JACKSON.

Scale of Miles.

Observations.

Lake George which was called by the French Lac du St. Sacrement
is named by the Indians Caniad-eri-oit, that is, Tail of the Lake.
It is bounded on both Sides with exceeding high Mountains: Its
Navigation is obstructed, at the Northern End, by a Ridge of Rocks
over which the Surplus Issue of its Waters Falls.
The Course which our Troops took, during the Last War was
generally to Land on Sabbath-Day Point, whence a
Road Leads to Ticonderago*.

* Topog: Descrip. p.13.
by Gov.r Pownall.

French Point
Sabbath Day Point
Point Pleasant

A. Fort William Henry, afterwards Fort George.
B. Bridge.
C. Lime Kilns.
D. Brick-Yard.
E. A Rising Ground that overlooks the Fort.
✗ Where Sr Wm Johnson defeated Genl Dieskau Sept 8th 1755.
N.B. The Figures denote Fathoms.

13

Lake George

Characteristics

Lake George is located in upstate New York, roughly equidistant between New York City to the south and Montreal to the north. It is about thirty-two miles in length, averages one and one-half miles in width, with a maximum depth of nearly 200 feet. It lies wholly within the Adirondack Park (see sidebar on page 16). The lake's surface is 317 feet above sea level and covers approximately 44.4 square miles. Lake George has 176 miles of shoreline and over 165 islands. Lost in any numerical description of Lake George however, is the sheer beauty that one observes when looking at the crystal clear waters dotted with small islands surrounded by precipitous elevations that rise 500 to over 2500 feet from the water.

Formation

The forces that created the lake can be traced back to Pre-Cambrian times, over 500 million years ago, when the region was a peneplain about to be covered with sea water. Throughout the Cambrian Period, the whole region slowly re-elevated to eventually become dry land once again and many of the mountain ridges visible today were thrust upward.

Most of the lakes, rivers, and streams that we see today however, are the result of much more recent geological events that occurred during the Glacial Period. The advance of the Labrador ice sheet over the region covered the area with ice over a half-mile thick. When the ice retreated, many higher grounds were scoured and the glacial deposits left behind filled in numerous low areas. What had once been two valley streams, one flowing north from what is known today as The Narrows, and the other flowing south from Northwest Bay, became a single lake filled with melting glacial ice. The glacial deposits left behind now block the southern discharge and force the flow of the lake northward to Ticonderoga, where its outlet, the La Chute River, descends over 200 feet before entering Lake Champlain.

Climate

Weather in the Lake George region varies drastically from season to season. July is the warmest month, with daytime highs averaging in the low-to-mid 80s. January is the coldest month, with daytime highs only around 20 degrees Fahrenheit. In both seasons temperature variations between night and day average about 25 degrees. This variation leads to cool summer nights and over-night winter temperatures that can fall below zero. Precipitation throughout the year is fairly consistent, averaging 3 ½ to 4 inches per month.

Weather

Boaters on Lake George need to be particularly mindful of the weather. Because of the funnel-like nature of Lake George with its high mountains and narrow basin, severe storms can arise suddenly, resulting in rough water and strong winds. Moreover, the lake's high mountains can block your view of approaching storms. Check weather forecasts often, watch the skies, and be prepared to seek shelter. NOAA and U.S.C.G. weather broadcasts can be received on VHF radio.

Getting Here

• **By Vehicle** — Lake George Village, which lies at the southern end of the lake, is easily accessed by interstate highway. From New York City and points south, one should get to the New York State Thruway (I-87) heading north and follow it to Albany. Leave the Thruway at Exit 24 and continue to follow I-87 north. Take Exit 21 and follow the signs into the village from the south. Travelers from Boston and points east should take the Massachusetts Turnpike (I-90) west, and continue to follow I-90 into New York State and onto the Thruway Spur, exit-ing at Exit B-1 (still following I-90). In Albany, take Exit 24 onto I-87 north to exit 21. From Buffalo and points west, I-90 crosses the state (New York State Thruway) into Albany, where exit 24 will take you to I-87 north and Exit 21. From Montreal and points north, follow Autoroute 15 south to the international border, where it becomes Interstate 87. Follow this highway south to Exit 22, and follow the signs into the village from the north.

• **By Airplane** — The closest major airport to Lake George Village is Albany International Airport. Taxis or airport shuttles can then transport you to Lake George Village. Private aircraft can land at Floyd Bennett Memorial Airport in nearby Queensbury which is less than 15 miles from the village.

• **By Train** — Amtrak offers service to Ft. Edward, NY on The Ethan Allen Express between Rutland, Vermont and New York City, and on The Adirondack between Montreal and New York City. Both trains make connections in Albany/Rensselaer for those people coming from the east or west. Travelers are urged to contact Amtrak directly for schedules (1-800-USA-RAIL). The Ft. Edward Amtrak station is located about 15 miles from Lake George Village.

Historical Background

Though tranquil today, few lakes in the country can rival the historically significant and often bloody past of Lake George. Because of its geography, Lake George served as a natural water route for Native Americans, and for Europeans after their arrival in the mid seventeenth century. During the 1700s Lake George played a key role in conflicts fought to determine control of the North American continent. Following the end of the American Revolution, the lake would become the playground for the rich and famous, and the resort destination that we know today as the "Queen of American Lakes."

Prehistory

Native Americans first came to Lake George over 10,000 years ago. Algonquin, Abenaki, Huron, Iroquois and others plied the waters of the lake that they called "Andia-ta-roc-te," or the place where the lake is shut in. Traveling in dugout or birch bark canoes, they used Lake George as a vital transportation link between Lake Champlain to the north and the Hudson River to the south. Archaeological evidence of their presence including pottery, projectile points, wampum, and hearths has been uncovered at several locations along Lake George's shoreline. Their presence is also reflected in many of the place names used today, such as Ticonderoga, Saratoga, Adirondack, and Kayaderosseras.

The Adirondack Park

The Adirondack Park was established in 1892 by the New York State Legislature in response to concerns the threat of the logging industry posed to the state's waterways of the day, namely the Hudson River and Erie Canal. It comprises an area of 6.1 million acres, which is greater than the entire nearby state of Vermont. It also exceeds the combined areas of Yellowstone, Grand Canyon, Everglades, and Glacier National Parks. The State of New York owns approximately 45% of the lands within the Park, with the balance being privately held. About 130,000 people live in the Park's 103 towns and villages. They share in the beauty and enjoyment of the 3000 lakes, 30,000 miles of rivers and streams, and 2000 miles of hiking trails found within the Park's boundaries. It is estimated that 7–10 million people visit the Park each year. Most of the State's holdings have been declared a "forever wild" forest preserve, with much of the privately-owned lands being used for agriculture, forestry, and outdoor recreation.

First Europeans

The first Europeans to explore the Lake George/Lake Champlain valley arrived in the early 17th century. In July of 1609, the French explorer Samuel de Champlain came down Lake Champlain accompanied by a Huron and Algonquin war party. At the peninsula of Ticonderoga at the outlet of Lake George, Champlain's party made contact with a band of Iroquois, blood enemies of the Huron. In the battle that ensued, Champlain killed three chiefs with a single shot from his arquebus. Startled by the thunder of the unknown weapons and foreigners in metal armor, the Iroquois fled into the forest. This event would set the tone of French-Iroquois relations for the next 150 years.

The first European to actually set eyes on Lake George was Father Isaac Jogues. Father Jogues was a French Jesuit missionary who had come to the new world in 1642 to preach Christianity to the Huron Indians. Soon after his arrival, Jogues was captured by an Iroquois war party and brought south to their villages along the Mohawk River near present-day Schenectady. After being repeatedly tortured, Jogues managed to escape and return to France only after being shipwrecked on the English coast. Four years later, Father Jogues was asked to return to the New World, this time as ambassador to the same Iroquois who had held him captive several years before. Nevertheless, Jogues agreed and arrived in the Iroquois villages in the fall of 1646. During this trip south, Jogues took the route passing down *Andiatarocte*. Seeing the lake for the first time, Jogues was awed by its beauty and named it "Lac Du Saint Sacrament," or "Lake of the Blessed Sacrament." Not long after his arrival to the Iroquois villages, Jogues was blamed for a famine and plague that devastated the village, and was killed. The Catholic Church canonized Jogues in the 1930s. The lake would hold the name Lac Du Saint Sacrament for over 100 years. (A statue of Father Jogues stands in Fort George Park at the lake's south end).

French and Indian War (1754–1763)

By the 1750s, growing tensions between the British colonies and the French to the north came to a head. Beginning in 1754, the French and Indian War (the Seven-Years War in Europe), was fought to determine who would control the North American continent. The keys to success were the strategic waterways of the Hudson River, Lake George and Lake Champlain. Together, this water route extended hundreds of miles from New York City to Canada and was the only way of transporting the massive armies of both sides. Lake George would soon become a battlefield.

By the fall of 1755, over 3,000 British regulars and American provincial troops under the command of General William Johnson had assembled on the south shore of the lake. William Johnson renamed the lake "Lake George" in honor of then reigning King George II. In response to the British presence on the lake, the French dispatched a force of French regulars, Canadian militia, and Indian allies and attacked the British on September 8 in what has become known as the Battle of Lake George (at the site of present-day Fort George Park and Battlefield Campground). Greatly outnumbered, the French force was defeated, and soon after, the British began construction of Fort William Henry on the south shore of the lake. Meanwhile, the French were building Fort Carillon on Lake Champlain at the outlet of Lake George. Lake George had become the line in the sand.

In 1757, the French General Marquis de Montcalm led an 8,000-man army comprised of French and Canadian troops, and Indian allies from as far away as the Mississippi, to dislodge the British and destroy Fort William Henry. Splitting his force, Montcalm's men moved down the lake both by land

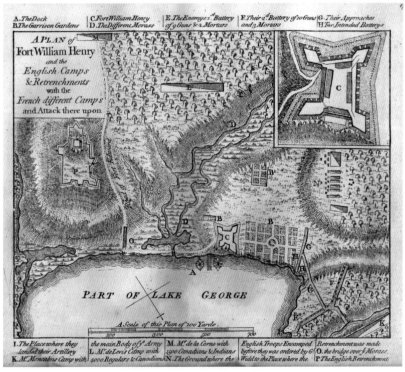

A Plan of Fort William Henry and the French Camps, 1756.

and by water, and by August 5, were laying siege to the Fort. By August 9, the 2,300 beleaguered British and Provincial American troops had no choice but to surrender to the French. In honor of their gallant defense of Fort William Henry, Montcalm allowed the paroled British garrison to march south to Fort Edward the following morning. However, Montcalm's Indians were furious at the release of the defeated British which denied them the customary spoils of war. As they began to march away, the Indians fell upon the terrified prisoners, scalping and killing all that resisted. The siege of Fort William Henry, and the resulting "massacre," was later made famous by James Fenimore Cooper's *Last of the Mohicans.*

The British responded the following year with the largest army ever to be assembled in North America until the Civil War. Leading the expedition was Major General James Abercromby, an uninspired officer given the derogatory nickname of "Granny" by many of the troops. This massive force of over 15,000 men set sail in early July from the south shore of Lake George in over 1,000 boats in columns that extended for miles along the lake. They landed at the north end of Lake George and marched for Fort Carillon. On July 8, the British and American provincials made a rash frontal attack on the hastily constructed French lines, built on high ground about a half-mile west of Fort Carillon. Led by the gallant 42nd Highland Regiment known as "The Black Watch," the British attackers were devastated by the withering French fire. Within hours, nearly 2,000 British soldiers had been killed or wounded. Despite outnumbering the French nearly 4 to 1, the panicked British and American provincial troops retreated to their boats on Lake George, and eventually returned to the lake's south end. They spent the remainder of the summer preparing for a French counter-attack that would never come.

As a result of that humiliating defeat in 1758, Major General Jeffery Amherst replaced Major General James Abercromby for the 1759 campaign against the French in the Champlain Valley. Known as the "Building General," Amherst was a methodical, careful planner who had led the successful assault against the French stronghold of Louisbourg the previous year. Soon after arriving, Amherst ordered the construction of several forts between Fort Edward and Lake George, including Fort George on the hill just south of present-day Million Dollar Beach. (Only the southwest bastion of the fort was ever completed.) By late July, Amherst's army of over 11,000 men set sail from the south end of Lake George in another attempt to capture Fort Carillon to the north. In contrast to the disaster of 1758, Amherst's methodical leadership paid off. The greatly out-numbered French evacuated Fort Carillon during the night of July 26 after blowing up the fort's magazines. From that time on, the fort would be known as Fort Ticonderoga. Amherst continued north driving French forces from the Champlain Valley, leading eventually to British control of Canada in 1763.

American Revolution (1775–1783)

The peace that descended over Lake George was short-lived. By 1775, the winds of war would again return to the lake with the start of the American Revolution. And again, Lake George would play a vital role in the conflict. Recognizing the importance of Lake George and Lake Champlain as an invasion route, the Americans, under the leadership of Benedict Arnold and Ethan Allen, seized forts Ticonderoga and Crown Point, and Fort George on Lake George. During that year, and into 1776, Lake George served as a staging area and supply route for the American army during its failed invasion of British Canada. In late fall of 1775 with the American Army heading north, Henry Knox sailed south on Lake George while transporting 59 cannon during his Herculean effort to deliver the guns to George Washington at Boston.

During the summer of 1777, the feared British invasion down the Lake Champlain valley came to pass. The British strategy was to advance south down Lake Champlain, Lake George, and the Hudson River and link up with British forces holding New York City. They believed that by gaining control of the Champlain/Hudson River water route, they could divide the American colonies in two, and ultimately end the war. By the fall of 1777, Lieutenant General John Burgoyne with an army of over 7,000 British and German soldiers had managed to advance to within 25 miles of Albany, New York. Behind him were supply lines extending hundreds of miles back to Canada, which included depots on Lake George at its north and south ends, as well as on Diamond Island.

An attempt was made to disrupt these supply lines on September 24, when the American Colonel John Brown and over 400 men in 20 boats attacked Diamond Island and its garrison of over 200 British and German troops. In what is now known as the "Battle of Diamond Island," Brown's force was repelled by the heavy British cannon on the island, and he was forced to retreat and burn his vessels in Dunham's Bay.

On October 17, 1777, Burgoyne and his entire force surrendered to the Americans after being defeated at the two battles of Saratoga. This vital American victory is considered the turning point of the Revolution, as its success brought the French and other European nations into the war on the American side, allowing us to ultimately secure our independence.

Rise of Lake George as a Tourist Destination

With a lasting peace finally brought to Lake George, tourists began to arrive on its beautiful shores. Some of the lake's earliest tourists included George Washington in 1783 and Aaron Burr in the early 1800s. One of the Lake George's greatest fans early on was Thomas Jefferson, who in 1791, wrote to his daughter that:

"Lake George is without comparison, the most beautiful water I ever saw; formed by a contour of mountains into a basin thirty-five miles long and from two to four miles broad, finely interspersed with islands, its water limpid as crystal and the mountainsides covered with rich groves of silver fir, white pine, aspen and paper birch down to the water, here and there precipices of rock to checker the scene and save it from monotony. An abundance of speckled trout, salmon trout, bass, and other fish with which it is stored, have added to our other amusements the sport of taking them."

By the early 1800s improvements in transportation made Lake George increasingly accessible to tourists. After 1817 steamboats began hauling freight and passengers up and down the lake. By 1825, stagecoach service made regular trips from Glens Falls to Lake George, only to be replaced by the railroad, which arrived at the lake in 1882.

To accommodate the rising tide of visitors made possible by these improvements, hotels and boarding houses began to spring up along the lake's shore. By the 1870s more than 20 hotels and boarding houses could be found in Caldwell (Lake George Village) alone. Some of these hotels were quite large and opulently appointed, including the Fort William Henry Hotel built in 1855 at the south end of the lake and the Sagamore Hotel, built in 1883 on Green Island near Bolton.

Much of the early success of Lake George as a tourist destination was due to the arrival of steamboats to the lake. In 1817, the 80-foot long *James Caldwell* was launched on Lake George. At a cost of $12,000 the ungainly little steamboat boasted a brick smoke stack and a 20 HP engine driving her to break-neck speeds of just under 5 miles per hour. It took an entire day to travel the length of Lake George. As the years passed, steamboats helped the lake communities to flourish, transporting thousands of tourists and tons of cargo each year to regularly scheduled stops along the lake. By their heyday in the late 1800s, Lake George steamboats reached lengths of over 200 feet and were capable of carrying over 1,700 passengers. Many of these elegant boats offered overnight staterooms, fine dining, music, entertainment, and even theatrical performances. Today, the excursion boats of Lake George are no longer driven by steam, but continue to grace the waters of the lake carrying thousands of visitors each year.

Millionaires Row

With the rise of American industry in the late 1800s came prosperity. Through skill, intelligence, luck, and often ruthlessness, individuals amassed enormous fortunes, and included names such as Rockefeller, Peabody, Trask, Vanderbilt, Singer, and Whitney. Much of this wealth was centered on the urban centers of the East including New York City, Philadelphia, and elsewhere. To escape the summer heat, many looked north to the Adirondacks and the shores of Lake George. Soon after the Civil War, millionaires began building opulent mansions along a 10-mile stretch of the west shore between Lake George Village and Bolton. This stretch became known as "Millionaires Row." Today, many of those mansions still tower over the lake, often the home to opulent resorts and restaurants. Listed below, are some of the surviving mansions beginning in Lake George Village and continuing north to Bolton.

Evelley

William J. Price built this English Tudor-style mansion at the end of the nineteenth century. Charles R. Peabody later purchased the home. Charles was a partner in the firm of Spencer Trask and invested heavily in American industry Charles was one of the three brothers who owned mansions on Millionaires Row.

Evelley. Mansion photos by Scott Padeni

22

The Quarters (Oak Lawn)

North of Evelley is The Quarters, which was the summer home of American photographer Alfred Stieglitz and his wife the American artist Georgia O'Keefe. The Quarters mansion is now the centerpiece of the Quarters Resort.

The Quarters

Rockledge

Rockledge is the oldest of the remaining mansions on Lake George today. The Victorian mansion was built in 1876 by the Reverend Dr. Isaac Tuttle. Dr. Tuttle was an Episcopal rector from New York City and arrived here in 1855. He also founded St. James Episcopal Church in the Village of Lake George.

Rockledge

Erlowest

Erlowest

This large stone mansion was the home of Edward Morse Shepard. Shepard was born July 23, 1850, and educated at CCNY where he graduated with honors at 19 years of age. He became a corporate lawyer with much of his wealth coming from holdings in mining and railroads. Shepard was a philanthropist and author, heavily involved in New York politics. Shepard died of pneumonia at Erlowest on July 20, 1911. The mansion, constructed in 1898, is Queen Anne in design and Baroque in decoration. It later became the home of Charles R. Wood, founder of the Great Escape amusement park, now known as Six Flags. After selling the mansion, Wood donated the money to the nearby Double H Hole in the Woods Camp for children with terminal illnesses, founded by Wood and Paul Newman approximately 25 years ago. The mansion now serves as the Erlowest Inn and Sun Castle Resort.

Blenheim on the Lake (Wikiosko)

Blenheim on the Lake is believed by many to be of the most beautiful of the mansions on Millionaires Row. Royal Peabody, founder of Brooklyn Edison, which later became Con Ed in New York City, built it in 1895 and named it Wikiosko, meaning the "House of Beautiful Waters." The mansion is English-Tudor revival in design, and is privately owned today.

Green Harbor: the Pitcairn Estate

The large mansion on Cooper Point was built around 1900, and is the largest of the remaining homes on Millionaires Row. It has 42 rooms, including 20 bedrooms and 10 bathrooms. The home was purchased by Frederick F. Peabody and was eventually sold to Harold Pitcairn in 1929. Harold was

Blenheim on the Lake   Green Harbor

heir to the Pittsburgh Plate Glass Company and one of the original develop-
ers of the autogyro, an aircraft similar to a helicopter. Today, the mansion is
privately owned and serves as a single family home.

Depe Dene

Captain D.S. Denison, an 1858 graduate of West Point, built Depe Dene. He
served in the army through the Civil War and retired in the 1880s. He purchased the 200-acre property in 1898 and built the main house. The footprint
of the mansion measures 60 ft by 60 feet. It is five stories tall with each floor
having balconies looking out over the lake. Depe Dene has ten bedrooms and
seven bathrooms and a 6,000-gallon fuel oil tank. An executive from Proctor
and Gamble once owned the home and it is said the recipe for Crisco was
invented here in the kitchen of this mansion.

Depe Dene

Stebbins
Mansion

Stebbins Mansion

The Stebbins home on Cannon Point was built in 1908 for sisters Louise and Anna Stebbins. The two sisters spent summers on the lake, though often rented the lavish mansion to prominent New York notables. In 1911, New York Governor John A. Dix rented the house for the summer. In 1925 Charles Evans Hughes rented the home. Mr. Hughes was born in 1862 in Glens Falls, and later became a prominent lawyer and politician. In 1906, he was elected Governor of New York, defeating William Randolph Hearst. In 1910 he became a United States Associate Justice, though he resigned from the court in 1916 to run for President of the United States as a Republican against Woodrow Wilson. Hughes lost in one of America's closest presidential elections. He then served as Secretary of State under Harding and Coolidge, and in 1930 President Hoover appointed him Chief Justice of the Supreme Court. He held that position until 1941. Charles Evans Hughes died on August 27, 1948. Today, the Stebbins mansion is part of the Cannon Point condominium complex.

Bixby Estate

The Bixby estate is situated on Mohican Point in Bolton Landing. William and Lillian (Tuttle) Bixby built the mansion in 1902, after tearing down the decaying Mohican House. The Mohican House was the first inn and tavern on the lake, built around 1800.

Bixby.

Hermstone

"Hermstone" ("The Rock")

"Hermstone" was built along the shores of Bolton Landing by Herman Broesel in 1903 employing over 300 stone masons. The home boasts 7000 square feet with 10 bedrooms. Broesel was a partner of the firm of Brossneck, Broesel and Co. as well as President of the Jefferson Bank, both of New York City. Broesel died in 1912 at the age of 54. Hermstone was later purchased by William Hoxie Bixby in 1935, and was renamed "The Rock."

For more information on Lake George History see:

Russell P. Bellico. *Chronicles of Lake George: Journeys in War and Peace,* Purple Mountain Press, Fleischmanns, NY, 1995.

Russell P. Bellico. *Sails and Steam in the Mountains,* Purple Mountain Press, Fleischmanns, NY, Revised Edition, 2001.

Kathryn E. O'Brien. *The Great and the Gracious on Millionaires Row: Lake George in its Glory.* Utica, New York: North Country Press.

William (Bill) Preston Gates has also written several histories on Lake George, including: *History of the Sagamore Hotel, Millionaires' Row on Lake George,* and *Old Bolton on Lake George, NY.* www.wpgates.com

The Cruise Boats of Lake George

For many visitors to the "Queen of American Lakes," their fondest memories are of the sight of grand cruise boats plying the crystal waters of Lake George, with their horn blasts echoing among the mountains. The cruise boats of today continue a rich legacy that dates back to the 19th century — the golden age of the Lake George steamer. The first Lake George steamboat was the *William Caldwell* built in 1817. Complete with a brick smokestack, the *Caldwell* was capable of speeds of up to 4 mph, allowing her to navigate the entire length of the lake in a single day. The *Caldwell* burned at her dock in 1821, but was followed by many others. By the late 1800s and early 1900s, some Lake George steamboats were upwards of 230 feet long, carrying over 1500 passengers.

So rugged is the terrain surrounding Lake George, that until the early 20th century, these vessels represented the only means of efficient transportation up and down the lake. But for many passengers, these vessels represented much more than mere transportation—they were an event. Many of these large steamers offered fine dining, casino gambling, theatrical performances, musical concerts, overnight accommodations, and even snake charmers! Among the ranks of their passengers included notables such as Francis Parkman, Ralph Waldo Emerson, Professor Benjamin Silliman, and Washington Irving.

The Lake George cruise boats of today continue to entertain thousands of passengers each year, though unlike their steam-powered predecessors, however, most of today's cruise boats are powered by diesel engines and electrical generators, and guided by satellite GPS, sonar, radar, and VHF communications. Only the graceful *Minne-Ha-Ha* continues to harness the power of steam.

Lac Du Saint Sacrement

The *Lac Du Saint Sacrement* is the largest of the cruise boats on Lake George today. Its name comes from the earlier French name for the lake, given to it in 1646 by the Jesuit Missionary Father Issacc Jogues.

The *Lac du Saint Sacrement.*
Photo by Scott Padeni

Lac Du Saint Sacrement **specifications:**

Owner: Lake George Steamboat Company
Construction: July 1978 through June 1989
Where built: Baldwin Shipyard, Ticonderoga, NY
Cost: $4,250,000 • **Length:** 189 feet • **Beam:** 40 feet • **Draft:** 7.5 feet
Displacement: 521 long tons • **Horsepower:** 1,350 • **Speed:** 15 knots
Passenger Capacity: 1,000

Adirondac

The *Adirondac* is the newest of the Lake George cruise boats operating on the lake today. Scarano Boat of Albany, NY designed this elegant passenger vessel to reflect the great steamboats of Lake George's golden age. This classic styled three-decker comes complete with rollaway sunroof and bridal suite.

The *Adirondac*.
Photo by Scott
Padeni

Adirondac **specifications:**

Owner: Shoreline Cruises
Construction: 2004 by Scarano Boat, Albany, NY
Where built: hull in Albany, NY. Completed on Lake George.
Length: 115 feet • **Beam:** 30 feet • **Draft:** 5 feet
Displacement: 136 Long tons
Horsepower: two John Deere diesels providing a total 1000 HP
Speed: 12 knots • **Passenger capacity:** 400

Mohican

The *Mohican* is the second passenger vessel to carry that name on Lake George. The first *Mohican* (I) was built in 1894. However her 93-foot wooden hull proved less durable than hoped, and in 1907 she was replaced by the steel hulled *Mohican* (II). Today, the *Mohican* is one of the longest serving passenger vessels in the country, and is listed on the National Register of Historic Places. She is only one of three passenger vessels to hold that honor.

The *Mohican*.
Photo by Scott
Padeni

Mohican specifications:

Owner: Lake George Steamboat Company
Construction: 1906–1907 by T.S. Marvel Shipbuilding Co., Newburgh, NY
Where built: Newburgh, NY. Dismantled and reassembled at
Baldwin Shipyard, Ticonderoga, NY • **Hull:** Steel • **Length:** 115 feet
Beam: 26.5 feet • **Draft:** 5 feet, 3 inches • **Displacement:** 200 tons •
Horsepower: twin Caterpillar diesels providing a total 760 HP
Speed: 15 knots • **Passenger capacity:** 130

Horicon

Today's *Horicon* is the third passenger vessel on the lake to carry the name. The first *Horicon* was built in 1877 and was 195 feet long with a 30-foot beam. In 1911, the larger steel-hulled *Horicon* (II) replaced the wooden-hulled *Horicon* (I). The second *Horicon* was 230 feet long with a beam of 59 feet, to this day the largest passenger vessel to ever operate on Lake George. While far smaller than her two ancestors, the present *Horicon* is the largest wood hulled vessel on the lake.

The *Horicon*.
Photo by Scott
Padeni

Horicon specifications:

Owner: Shoreline Cruises
Construction: 1988 by Scarano Boat Albany NY
Where built: Hull in Albany, NY. Completed on Lake George.
Hull: Composite (Fiberglass over wood)
Length: 88 feet • **Beam:** 22 feet • **Draft:** 4 feet • **Displacement:** 97 long tons
Horsepower: twin Cummins diesels providing a total 500 HP
Speed: 12 knots • **Passenger capacity:** 150

Morgan

What the *Morgan* may lack in size, she compensates for with style, boasting classic lines, mahogany upper works, and bronze portholes. Built on Green Island by Morgan Marine in 1985, the *Morgan* serves as the centerpiece for the Sagamore Resort in Bolton. Countless weddings and other functions are conducted on this vessel each year, with the beauty of the Narrows as their backdrop.

The *Morgan*.
Photo by Scott
Padeni

Morgan specifications:

Owner: Sagamore Resort
Construction: 1985–1986 by Morgan Marine, Silver Bay, Lake George
Where built: Green Island, Bolton Landing, NY
Hull: Composite (Fiberglass over plywood)
Length: 72 feet • **Beam:** 26 feet • **Draft:** 5 feet • **Displacement:** 80 tons
Horsepower: single diesel providing 250 HP • **Speed:** 12 knots
Passenger capacity: 130

Minne-Ha-Ha

Of all the Lake George cruise boats, the *Minne-Ha-Ha* is without question the most iconic. Few Lake George brochures can be found without an image of the Minne with her paddlewheel churning the lake's water. Her name "Minne-Ha-Ha" means "Laughing Water", and was the name given to the wife of the famous Indian Chief Hiawatha. Her design is that of the classic paddlewheel Mississippi River boats of the 19th century and is the only steam powered cruise boat on Lake George today. The "Minne," as she is affectionately referred to, even has a steam-powered calliope producing patriotic songs that echo off the surrounding mountains. She is the second *Minne-Ha-Ha* on the lake. The first vessel using that name was built in 1857 and operated until 1877. Due to the popularity of today's *Minne-Ha-Ha*, she was lengthened from her original 103 feet to her present length of 137 feet. Her steam engine produces 6,000 lbs. of steam per hour to turn her 12-foot diameter stern paddlewheel.

The *Minne-ha-ha*. Photo by Scott Padeni

Minne-ha-ha specifications:

Owner: Lake George Steamboat Company
Construction: 1969 by Lake George Steamboat Company
Where built: Baldwin Shipyard, Ticonderoga, NY
Hull: Steel
Length: 137 feet
Beam: 30 feet
Draft: 3.5 feet
Displacement: 250 tons

Lake George Wildlife

By Emily DeBolt, courtesy the Lake George Association.

Mammals

A few small mammals can be commonly found swimming along the shorelines of Lake George.

Beaver (Castor canadensis)

North America's largest rodent and New York's official state mammal, the beaver is recognized by its smooth brown coat and large black, flattened, paddle-shaped tail. With waterproof fur, webbed hind feet and the ability to hold its breath for 15 minutes, the beaver is well adapted to life in the water. Growing up to 46" long and an average weight of 45-60 pounds, the beaver is also known for its large chestnut-colored incisors it uses to gnaw bark, twigs and fell trees. A single beaver can chew down hundreds of trees each year. Builders of dams and large stick lodges, they can alter the landscape, turning a stream into a vast marshland habitat. Beavers can be seen swimming in the evening along the shores of Lake George.

Otter (Lontra canadensis)

River otters have a dark brown, elongated body with a large, thick tail and webbed feet. The river otter is found along rivers, ponds and lakeshores where it will forage mainly for fish. In murky water, they can find their prey by sensing vibrations with their whiskers. They will often hunt in pairs, driving a school of small fish into an inlet where they can be easily caught. They will also eat small mammals

Beaver. Photo by Magnus Manske, Wikipedia

Otter. Photo by Scott Padeni

33

such as mice and terrestrial invertebrates. The otter is a swift and agile swimmer, using its muscular tail to make sharp turns and steering with its neck and webbed feet. It swims rapidly like a flexible torpedo both underwater and on the surface and is noted for its playful antics and "slides" on land and in the snow. Otters can be seen in the northern end of the lake, in the Huletts Landing area.

Muskrat (Ondatra zibethicus)
The muskrat is a large vole-like rodent with dense glossy, dark brown fur and a long scaly tail. Its scaly, laterally compressed tail with a fringe of coarse hair along the underside is a feature muskrats share with no other New York State mammal. Living along streams, lakes or marshy areas, they make houses similar to beaver lodges, only made of cattails, grasses and plant material rather than sticks. Muskrats eat primarily aquatic vegetation such as cattails and pondweed, but will also eat freshwater clams, fish and frogs. Muskrat can be seen swimming along the shores of the lake, and often leave behind piles of empty mussel shells in boathouses.

White Tailed Deer (Odocoileus virginianus)
White-tailed deer can be found from southern Canada to South America. Their habitat is typically open fields and meadows during the summer months, while the forests during the winter months offer protection from the elements. Their coats are usually reddish-brown fading to a gray-brown in the winter. Bucks, or male deer, grow antlers during the summer months that fall off during the coming winter. These antlers are used to spar with competing bucks over territory or potential mates. Around May or June female deer, known as does, give birth to as many as three fawns that are recognizable by their reddish brown fur and

Muskrat. The United States Fish and Wildlife Service

White Tailed Deer. Photo by Scott Padeni

white spots that help camouflage them in the forest. White-tailed deer are herbivores with the ability to survive on a large variety of plants. These animals are most often seen on the move at dusk or dawn.

Birds

Many birds make the lake their major source of food (fish, frogs, crustaceans, aquatic plants, etc.) and find the shoreline habitat a primary place for foraging, roosting and nesting.

Bald Eagle (Haliaeetus leucocephalus)

Bald eagles are the National Bird of the United States. Although they were almost extinct by 1950 from the effects of DDT and other environmental pollutants, they rebounded and were de-listed from the Federal Endangered and Threatened Wildlife List in 2007. Bald eagles prefer a habitat near large bodies of open water with an abundance of fish for their main diet. They also require that this habitat have mature stands of trees nearby for perching, roosting and nesting with good visibility and proximity to prey. Nests are reused and added to each year, growing to over six feet across, eight feet deep and weighing hundreds of pounds. Although eagles live mainly on fish, they are opportunistic feeders and will supplement with carrion, small mammals such as rabbits, raccoons and young beavers as well as other birds like ducks and geese. An eagle's 2-inch-long talons can exert 1,000 pounds of pressure per square inch. In recent years they have been spending a lot of time on Lake George and Lake Champlain; even in the winter, these semi-migratory birds have chosen to remain where there has been open water for feeding on fish and ducks in ice-free areas.

Bald Eagle. The United States Fish and Wildlife Service

Peregrine Falcon. The United States Fish and Wildlife Service

Peregrine Falcon (Falco peregrinus)

Flying high and circling until prey is spotted, then a swooping dive of over 100 miles per hour to strike the prey right out of the air, the peregrine falcon is one of the world's fastest and most spectacular birds of prey. The peregrine falcon was seriously endangered in the mid-20th century due to the effects of DDT and other pesticides. Reintroduction efforts have been successful and over the last 20 years the numbers of nesting pairs has risen steadily. In 1991, the first nesting pair of peregrine falcons nested on Anthony's Nose at the northern end of Lake George. Since then, the offspring of this first pair have established at least 2 or 3 other sites — one of the most successful is across the lake on the cliffs of Rogers Rock. Falcons prefer cliff ledges for their nesting sites; and the dramatic calcareous cliffs of Lake George offer that and access to an abundant food supply made up of fairly large birds such as ducks and geese, gulls and small mammals.

Great Blue Heron (Ardea herodias)

The great blue heron stands about four feet tall on stilt-like legs. It has a long neck and a white head with two black crown stripes with a long, yellow bill ideal for snatching or spearing the frogs, snakes and fish that make up its diet. A heron in flight is impressive. The head and neck stretch out forward during take-off and then are retracted into an "S" shape while cruising. A six-foot wingspan helps them glide close to the water, traveling up to five miles from the rookery in search of food. Difficult to notice when they are not flying, herons will stand completely still, their colors blending into the rocky shoreline, waiting to surprise unwary prey. It is worthwhile to visit the LGLC Gull Bay Preserve in Putnam to take in the heron rookery where their large stick nests and families can be observed in an abandoned beaver pond near the lake.

Great Blue Heron. Photo by Scott Padeni

Gull. The United States Fish and Wildlife Service

Gulls (family Laridae).

Out on the lake we can observe birds in the gull family. They spend their time either flying over the water in search of small fish to eat, floating in the open water or gathered in groups on small rocky islands. On Lake George we can find the Herring Gull, Ring-billed Gull and Great Black-backed Gull. Sometimes called seagulls, these birds are protected in NY State.

Double Crested Cormorant (Phalacrocorax auritus)

Double crested cormorants are fish-eaters preferring smaller varieties like smelt and young trout and bass that live in shallow water depths of 25 feet or less. Visual predators, they must be able to see the fish underwater to catch them and our clean lake does give them some advantage, as they are able to chase a fish to a depth of 60 feet! There has been some concern over possible impacts on sport fishing, but with most of Lake George much deeper than they can forage, these excellent divers and swimmers are confined to only a few islands for roosting. There is a small, non-breeding population here on Lake George but the DEC is closely monitoring and managing them to make sure that there are no more than 20 birds residing here and no nesting birds at all.

Common Loon (Gavia immer)

This icon of the Adirondacks is known for its laugh-like trembling call heard across still waters. Loons are large swimming birds that dive underwater to forage on small fish, crustaceans and other aquatic life. These birds exhibit a behavior called "peering" which is characterized by the birds swimming with their eyes and bill submerged underwater to locate prey before they dive. Loons can dive at least 100 feet and normally remain underwater for about one minute, but

Double Crested Cormorant. Wikimedia Commons, Author: MDF

Common Loon. Photo by John Picken

sometimes remain submerged for up to three minutes. Loons' only significant competitors for lake habitat are humans. Boaters, shoreline development, intrusive anglers and recreationalists are threats to loons when nesting and raising the one or two chicks they hatch each year. Babies will spend 65% of their first week riding on their parent's back to increase their chance of survival. Human interaction has impacted the loon in other ways. In the late 1800s loons were considered great "sport shooting" and although this is no longer a practice, the lead sinkers used by anglers became a modern threat to their existence. Loons pick up pebbles from the bottom to aid in digestion and lead sinkers can be ingested by mistake. Lead poisoning was attributed to up to 50% of all loon mortalities; consequently, lead sinkers were banned in 2004 to alleviate this devastation. Mercury pollution, which is carried to the Adirondacks from coal-burning power plants in the mid-west, is still a major threat to loons. Despite these challenges, the loon is surviving and recovering in New York State, in large part due to the Adirondack Cooperative Loon Program.

Please refrain from disturbing loons. To observe, use binoculars or your camera lens from a distance.

Common Merganser (Mergus merganser)

The common merganser has a sleek, elongated appearance, reaching 2' in length. The males have a glossy, dark green head while the females have a distinct reddish-brown head with a swept back crest. Fast swimmers and excellent divers, mergansers are often seen with their eyes and bill submerged in water searching for small fish and minnows before diving. Preferring shallow water of six feet or less, sometimes groups of mergansers will cooperatively drive schools of fish into shallower areas for easier foraging. Broods are large, and sometimes

Common Merganser. The United States Fish and Wildlife Service

Mallard. The United States Fish and Wildlife Service

females will lay eggs in each other's nests or abandon the ducklings before they can fly, resulting in mixed broods of up to 20 ducklings guided by a single remaining hen. Common mergansers are late migrants, only going as far south as needed to find large bodies of open water.

Mallard (Anas platyrhynchos)

The mallard is the most abundant duck in North America. Drakes (male ducks) are best distinguished by their green, iridescent heads and white neck ring. Overall, the drake has a grayish body with a brown chest and yellow bill. Females are streaked brown with a whitish tail and a yellowish-orange bill. In flight, a bluish-violet wing patch outlined in white help to identify the mallard. These ducks will migrate in large flocks, but will stick around wherever there is open water and are commonly seen here throughout the winter.

Wood Duck, Bufflehead, and American Black Duck are also found on Lake George, as are Canada Geese. Efforts are made to deter the geese from nesting and taking up residence on the beaches and shorelines since they have become a nuisance species, but migrating flocks in their V-shaped formations and occasional visitors are a welcome sight.

Reptiles

Northern Map Turtle (Graptemys geographica)

This is an aquatic turtle with an oval carapace that is covered by a network of dark-bordered yellow-orange lines and circles resembling the contour lines of a topographical map. Map turtles are "big water" inhabitants, primarily found in large lakes or rivers. Males (3.5"–7") rarely basking more than a few body

Northern
Map Turtle

39

lengths from the water, and the larger females (7"–11"), can live to at least 20 years. Map turtles feed underwater mornings and evenings primarily on snails, thin-walled mussels, crayfish, aquatic insects, algae and vegetation. Raccoons are the most significant predator on northern map turtle nests, whereas herons and large fish prey on hatchlings. These turtles are excellent swimmers and are quick to retreat when approached; however, they cannot escape the waterfront development that destroys nesting habitats, increased traffic mortality on females searching for nesting sites, speedboat propellers or hooks of bait fishermen. The NY State Comprehensive Wildlife Conservation Strategy lists them as a species of greatest conservation need.

Eastern Painted Turtle (Chrysemys picta)

This turtle has a smooth oval shell with red markings (painted) on the margins of the shell and over the yellow-striped neck. Males have longer foreclaws and a longer thicker tail than the larger females turtles. Eastern painted turtles grow to 4.5"–"6 inches long, living up to 35 years in the wild. They are found in soft-bottomed, slow-moving ponds, lakes or marshes with aquatic vegetation and sunny basking sites where they forage day and night for a wide range of vegetation, insects and crustaceans. Often seen basking in large populations, painted turtles are considered common in NY State.

Snapping Turtle (Chelydra serpentina)

The snapping turtle has a large, serrated rear carapace (upper shell) with a tail that has three rows of scales and a fleshy plastron (underside). These are large turtles, growing from 8"–14" and weighing up to 35 pounds. They have been known to live 35 years in the wild, preferring slow moving, shallow water with

Eastern Painted Turtle. The U. S. Fish and Wildlife Service

Snapping Turtle. The United States Fish and Wildlife Service

emergent vegetation where they will rest in warm shallows, often partially buried in the mud with only their eyes and nostrils exposed. They are underwater feeders that will feed on carrion, insects, fish, vegetation and even baby ducks! Their "snapping" jaws are powerful protection on land and can sever human fingers in self-defense. Never pick up a snapping turtle by its tail as you can sever its spinal cord, instead pick it up firmly by the rear flanges of the carapace and hold it away from your body. These turtles are indicator species for accumulative ecotoxins and are considered a species of greatest concern by the NY State Comprehensive Wildlife Conservation Strategy.

Northern Watersnake (Nerodia sipedon)

This snake is the only dark, relatively large and heavily bodied snake found in aquatic habitats. Adult northern watersnakes measure from 24"–42" inches in length. The best field markings are brown or reddish-brown cross bands and blotches on a tan, brown or gray background. The front half of the body is typically banded, whereas the back half is blotched. The belly is light with distinct reddish-brown crescent-shaped blotches, and many New York specimens have thin red stripes on the face. These snakes are the most aquatic snake in New York and can be found in almost any permanent freshwater locale. During the spring and fall, these snakes are most active in the day, becoming more nocturnal during the summer months. Northern water snakes are excellent swimmers, both on the surface and while submerged foraging along the water's edge or moving through the water in search of prey. They eat mainly fish and frogs, salamanders and tadpoles but also take small mammals, birds, juvenile turtles, insects and crayfish. Predators include hawks, herons, snapping turtles and large predatory fish like bass and northern pike.

Northern Watersnake. Photo by C.M. Parker

Timber Rattlesnake. Photo Wikipedia.

Timber Rattlesnake (Crotalus horridus)

Timber rattlesnakes are very large snakes ranging in size from 3' to just under 5' in length. They are also the largest venomous snakes in New York State. Two color schemes are commonly found on these snakes. The first consists of black or dark brown crossbands on a background of yellow, gray, or brown. The second color scheme found consists of dark crossbands on an even darker background. The snake is also covered with ridged scales causing a very rough appearance to its skin. The head of the timber rattlesnake is broad and triangular with smaller scales on the head bordered by larger scales.

The timber rattlesnake is a member of the pit viper family, and as such, has a small opening or pit below the eye on each side of the face. This sensory organ is heat sensitive and assists in detecting prey or potential enemies. As per their name, these snakes also have rattles on the ends of their tails. These rattles are sounded whenever the snake feels threatened or disturbed.

The rattlesnakes of New York are active between late April and October, though are not fully active until May. Mating occurs during the spring and fall, with the males often traveling miles following pheromones, or scents emitted by females. Females typically give birth to 4–14 young every three to five years that measure around one foot in length. Males mature within 5 years, with females reaching adulthood at between 7 and 10 years. These snakes can live up to 30 years. They shed their skins every year or two, each time adding an additional segment to the rattle on their tails.

Using their venom to immobilize prey, timber rattlesnakes feed on small mammals, birds, frogs, and even other snakes. These snakes are timid and generally avoid humans, but if you are bitten their venom can be fatal if not treated.

Timber rattlers prefer the rugged terrain and rocky ledges that the Adirondacks offer. However, their populations have been greatly depleted over the years due to diminishing habitats, development, hunting, and bounties that were paid for each rattlesnake killed. These bounties were outlawed by the State of New York in 1971.

Source (Northern Rattlesnake): NY State DEC, online at: http://www.dec.ny.gov/animals/7147.html

Camping, Picnicking, and Hiking

Camping

For many boaters camping is one of the greatest attractions of Lake George. Options abound, ranging from large traditional campgrounds with numerous amenities, to remote single site islands. What better way to enjoy the beauty of Lake George than on an island campsite deep in the Narrows, or sipping a glass of wine on your boat while staying at one of many cruiser sites. Hundreds of campsites are available on Lake George, maintained by New York State Department of Environmental Conservation (NYS DEC).

Island Sites

Camping on Lake George's Islands is a unique experience. Unlike conventional campsites, each island site is only accessible by boat. Island campers generally launch their boats and park their vehicles and trailers at the closest private marina. Fees for launch and parking vary. Each site comes with a dock, fireplace, privy, and picnic table. Most of the sites are private and well forested. Some of the smaller islands have a single campsite only, allowing you the luxury of enjoying your own private island. Campers must be at least 18 years of age to rent a site. Most sites allow a maximum of 6 campers per site. Unfortunately you'll have to leave Fido home.

Dogs are prohibited from any of the islands, their docks, and from boats tied up to those docks.

A total of 387 island campsites are spread across the entire lake on 44 state-owned islands. These island sites are organized into three groups, each with its own headquarters to make registration more convenient. You can also register at Norowal Marina in Bolton Landing (518-644-9125) between 9:30 am to 6:00 pm, except on Wednesdays and Thursdays. The cost of an island site is $28.00 per night, plus a $3.00 surcharge for trash removal. See locations on pages 76–79.

The **Long Island Group** is located on the southern portion of the lake only 5 miles north of Lake George Village. All 90 campsites in this group are located on the 100-acre Long Island. Camping on this island is often preferred by those wanting to be in close proximity to the attractions of Lake George Village. Nearby boat launches are plentiful on both the east and west shores of the lake. Long Island camping closes October 11. The ranger station is located in a small bay on the east side of the island and can be contacted at: (518) 656-9426.

The **Glen Island Group** includes island campsites in the central portion of Lake George including the Narrows. There are a total of 212 campsites in this group. Of these, 42 are designated as cruiser sites and are located in Red Rock Bay (30) and on Log Bay Island (12). Cruiser sites are reserved for vessels with sleeping quarters aboard. No tents are allowed. Each cruiser site comes with a fireplace and privy. Twenty-five of the Glen Island Group sites are actually located on the west shore, but are only accessible by boat. The ranger station overseeing the Glen Island Group is located on Glen Island in the Narrows. It is also home to Neuffer's Store. Glen Island camping closes October 11. You can contact the ranger station at (518) 644-9696.

The **Narrow Island Group** (Mother Bunch) is located in the vicinity of Huletts Landing roughly halfway up the lake. A total of 81 sites on 17 islands are available in this group. Nearby boat launches are located in Huletts Landing on the east shore, and at Silver Bay on the west shore. The ranger station overseeing this group of islands is located on Narrow Island near Huletts Landing. They can be contacted at (518) 499-1288. Narrow Island camping closes October 11.

Mainland Campgrounds

Three mainland campgrounds are available to campers on Lake George. Rogers Rock and Hearthstone campgrounds are on the lakeshore. Lake George Battlefield Campground is located in Lake George Village, a quarter mile south of Million Dollar Beach. Each of these campgrounds is accessible by car. Camping fees for these campgrounds is $22.00 per night.

Hearthstone Campground (518-668-5193) is located 2 ½ miles north of the Village on the lake's west shore. For a fee of $22 per night, Hearthstone offers 251 tent and trailer sites, hot showers, flush toilets, sand beach with life guard and a designated swimming area. There are no boat launch facilities, docks, or moorings. Hearthstone Campground closes September 26.

Rogers Rock Campground (and Waltonian Islands) (518-585-6746) is located in the Town of Hague at the north end of the lake. The campground has 332 campsites, ten of which are located on the Waltonian Islands near Friends Point. Amenities include 2 group camping areas; picnic area with tables, picnic pavilion rentals, fireplaces, flush toilets, hot showers, boat launch, mooring buoys, boat pump out facilities, large sand beach with lifeguards, and bathhouse. Camping fees are $22 per night. Moorings are $15 per day.

Lake George Battleground Campground (518-668-3348) is located in Lake George Village on the site of the Battle of Lake George fought in 1755. The campground is adjacent to the Battlefield Park and its many historical attractions and interpretive trail. This campground is also a short walk to Million Dollar Beach, shopping, restaurants, excursion boats, and other attractions of the Village. Amenities include 62 tent and trailer sites, hot showers, and flush toilets. This campground is not on the lakeshore, and consequently not boat accessible.

Day-Use Picnic Sites

There are 116 day-use picnic sites available on eight island and two mainland locations on the lake. Day-use picnicking is also available at Hearthstone and Rogers Rock campgrounds. Permits must be obtained on a first-come, first-serve basis at the headquarters for the region in which the site is located. Picnickers are charged by the boat to include up to nine people. All day-use sites close at 9:00 PM. Amenities on the day-use sites include docks, charcoal grills, fireplaces, and tables. Nine picnic shelters capable of holding up to 15 people are also available. Dogs are NOT permitted on any of the day-use island sites. The fee for day-use is $10 per boat per day.

Day-use islands in the Long Island group include: O.D. Heck and Diamond Islands; Hazel and Sarah Islands in the Glen Island Group; West Dollar, Odell, and Picnic Islands in the Narrow Island Group (Mother Bunch). Rogers Rock Campground administers day-use for Asas Island in the Waltonian Islands in Hague. Mainland day-use picnic sites are located at Black Mountain Point and Commission Point. The Glen Island headquarters administers both. For more information on day-use sites contact the applicable regional headquarters:

45

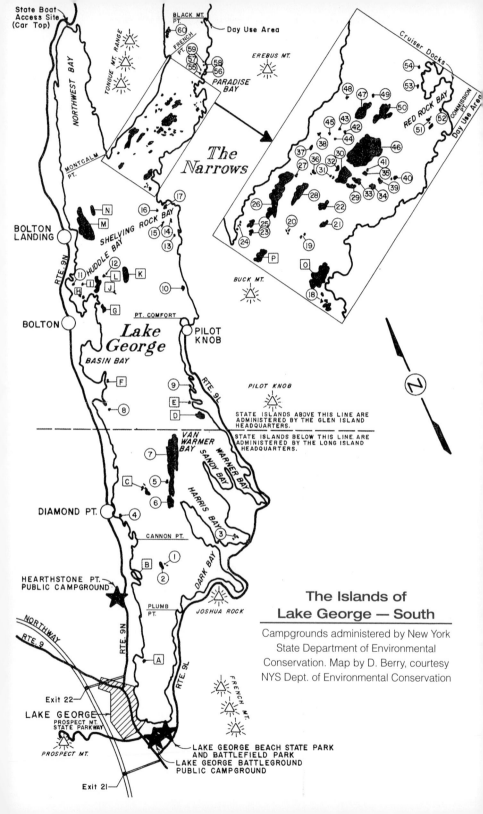

The Islands of
Lake George — South

Campgrounds administered by New York
State Department of Environmental
Conservation. Map by D. Berry, courtesy
NYS Dept. of Environmental Conservation

STATE OWNED ISLANDS :

I. Dicks (Pix) (2)	✴ 32. Brush
△✴ 2. Diamond	✴ 33. Phantom (Fantom)
3. Happy Family Group (5)	✴ 34. Gravelly
4. Fishook	✴ 35. Gem
5. Goose	36. Pleasure
△✴ 6. Speaker Heck	✴ 37. Bass (Perch)
✴ 7. Long	38. No Name (Bass)
8. Rush	✴ 39. Hermit
9. Whipple	✴ 40. Watch
✴ 10. Phelps (Little Ivanhoe)	41. Little Gem
11. Sweetbriar (Huckleberry)	✴ 42. Gourd
12. Little Recluse	✴ 43. Little Gourd
✴ 13. Refuge	44. The Coop (College Group)
14. Iroquois	(9)
✴ 15. Perch	45. Little As-You-Were
✴ 16. Huckleberry	✴ 46. Big Burnt
✴✴ 17. Log Bay	✴ 47. Little Harbor
✴ 18. Hen and Chickens Group (5)	48. As-You-Were
19. Bouquet	49. Black Rock
20. Ship	✴ 50. Fork (Kettle)
✴ 21. Ranger	✴ 51. Commission (Group) (3)
✴ 22. Juanita (Centipede)	52. Arrow
✴ 23. Pine	53. Red Rock
24. Mingoe	54. Artists Rock
25. Chingachagook (Little Pine)	(Round Rock)
✴ 26. Turtle	△✴ 55. Sarah (Chastine)
27. Little Turtle	△✴ 56. Hazel
✴ 28. Mohican (Pleasure, Phelps)	57. Unnamed (East of Hazel)
✴ 29. Glen	✴ 58. Fox
✴ 30. Uncas	59. Little Fox
✴ 31. Sunny	✴ 60. Dollar Group (3)
	61. Three Sirens (3)

✴ Docks   ✴✴ Cruiser Docks   △ Day Use Area

Note: Hen and Chickens Group & Commission Group
only 1 island has a dock. In the Dollar Group 2
islands have a dock. West Dollar-Day Use, East Dollar-camping

PRIVATELY OWNED ISLANDS :

A. Tea	I. Leantine (Little Whortleberry)
B. Coopers Point	
C. Canoe (3) (Three Sisters)	J. Clay (Belvoir)
D. Elizabeth (Little Green)	K. Dome
E. Triplets (3)(Near Travis Pt.)	L. Recluse (Picnic)
F. Cotton (Colton)	M. Green
G. Three Brothers (3)	N. Crown (Hog)
(Triuna, Three Sisters)	O. Fourteen Mile
H. Hiawatha	P. Bellingers, (Floa, Flea, Flora, Oahu)

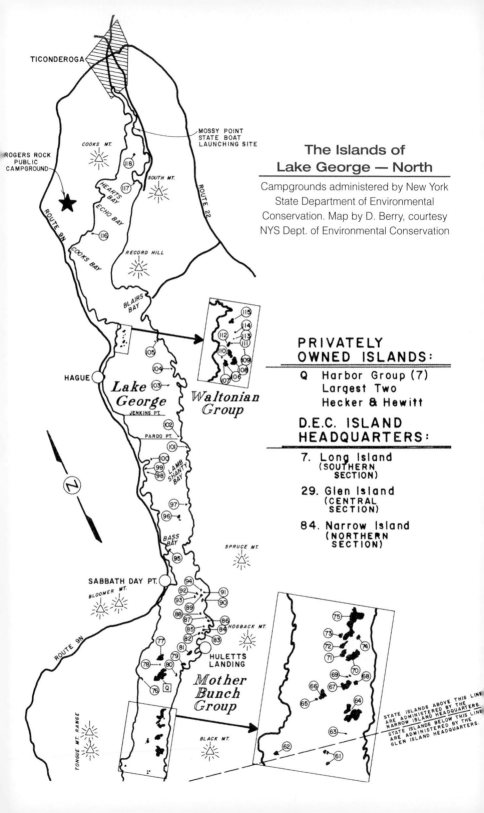

TICONDEROGA

MOSSY POINT
STATE BOAT
LAUNCHING SITE

COOKS MT.

ROGERS ROCK
PUBLIC
CAMPGROUND

SOUTH MT.

HEARTS BAY

ECHO BAY

ROUTE 22

ROUTE 9N

COOKS BAY

RECORD HILL

BLAIRS BAY

The Islands of
Lake George — North

Campgrounds administered by New York
State Department of Environmental
Conservation. Map by D. Berry, courtesy
NYS Dept. of Environmental Conservation

HAGUE

Lake
George

JENKINS PT.

Waltonian
Group

PARDO PT.

LAMB
SHANTY
BAY

BASS BAY

SPRUCE MT.

SABBATH DAY PT.

BLOOMER MT.

ROUTE 9N

HOGBACK MT.

HULETTS
LANDING

Mother
Bunch
Group

TONGUE MT. RANGE

BLACK MT.

PRIVATELY
OWNED ISLANDS:

Q Harbor Group (7)
    Largest Two
    Hecker & Hewitt

D.E.C. ISLAND
HEADQUARTERS:

7. Long Island
    (SOUTHERN
    SECTION)

29. Glen Island
    (CENTRAL
    SECTION)

84. Narrow Island
    (NORTHERN
    SECTION)

STATE ISLANDS ABOVE THIS LINE
ARE ADMINISTERED BY THE
NARROW ISLAND HEADQUARTERS.
STATE ISLANDS BELOW THIS LINE
ARE ADMINISTERED BY THE
GLEN ISLAND HEADQUARTERS.

STATE OWNED ISLANDS :

62. Halfway
63. One Tree
* 64. Floating Battery Group (4) (2 islands with docks)
65. Raggedy
* 66. Hatchet
* 67. Duran
* 68. Phenita (Fanita)
* 69. Little Burgess
* 70. Sagamore
△* 71. Picnic
* 72. Horicon
* 73. Unnamed - Mother Bunch No. 8
* 74. Coopers (Pine)
* 75. St. Sacrement
* 76. Steere (Sturgis)
* 77. Vicars
78. Unnamed (South of Vicars)
* 79. Nobles (Cooks)
80. Unnamed (2) (Near Nobles)
* 81. Burgess
82. Huletts (Whale)
83. Unnamed (Near Huletts)
* 84. Narrow
85. Rabbit Rock (Near Narrow)
86. Rock Dunder
87. Unnamed (Near Rock Dunder)
88. Loon
* 89. Agnes
90. Little Gibralter
91. Summer House Rock
92. Unnamed (Near Agnes)
93. Unnamed (Near Agnes)
94. Gillette (Allette)
95. Delaware (Watch)
△* 96. Odell (2) (1 island with dock)
97. Racket (North of Odell Group)
98. Skippers Jib
99. Pudding
100. Scotch Bonnet
101. Clark
* 102. Mallory
103. Gull
104. Crow
105. Rock Brothers (2)
* 106. Temple Knoll (Temple Noe, Watrous)
107. Unnamed (West of Temple Knoll)
* 108. Waltonian
109. Unnamed (North of Waltonian)
△* 110 Asas
111. Unnamed (Near Lenni - Lenape)
112. Lenni - Lenape (Lenawee, Cooks)
113. Unnamed (North of Lenni - Lenape)
114. Unnamed (South of Flirtation)
* 115. Flirtation
116. Juniper
117. Unnamed (South of Black Pt.)
118. Prison (Prisoners)

49

- Long Island Group Ranger Station: 518-656-9426
- Glen Island Group Ranger Station: 518-644-9696
- Narrow Island Group Ranger Station: 518-499-1288
- Rogers Rock Campground: 518-585-6746

Reserving a Campsite

Campsites fill up very quickly on Lake George, so it is highly recommended that you make reservations as early as possible, online at: http://newyork-stateparks.reserveamerica.com/camping or by contacting Reserve America at 1-800-456-2267. Have at least two choices in mind when you call.

Due to the recent threat posed by the invasive Asian Longhorned Beetle and Emerald Ash Borer, strict regulations have been established for the transportation of firewood. For details, go to: www.dec.ny.gov/animals/28722.html. For general camping rules and regulations, go to: www.dec.ny.gov/outdoor/7817.html

Hiking

Hiking is one of the top pastimes for those visiting Lake George. Hikes to the surrounding peaks offer breathtaking views of the lake, waterfalls and historic sites. There are over 50 miles of marked trails around the lake that are maintained by the NYS DEC, marked by red, blue or yellow markers. Several of these trails are boat accessible including Tongue Mountain and French Mountain trails on the west side of the lake, and Black Mountain and Shelving Rock trails on the east side of the lake. NY State dockage is available at Montcalm Point (Tongue Mountain trail) and at Black Mountain Point.

Always let someone know of your hiking itinerary, and take adequate safety precautions. Watch the weather, and dress properly for the conditions. When hiking on the Tongue Mountain Range, beware of Timber rattlesnakes that are found in that area.

For more information on Lake George hiking trails and safety precautions go to: www.dec.ny.gov/outdoor/9195.html.

Boating Information, Regulations, and Safety

Navigation

Pilotage through unfamiliar waters is always one of the greatest concerns of any boater. However, with some advanced preparation, the proper equipment, good seamanship, and a little common sense, boating in Lake George is not difficult.

While Lake George has its fair share of submerged hazards and shoals, the vast majority of them are clearly marked. Provided you take the time to study their location on available nautical charts, and the meaning of the lake's navigational markers and lights, boating on Lake George will be very enjoyable. Your most important tools when on the lake are your eyes — and your common sense. Remember that shoals and other hazards are often found close to the shoreline, between adjacent islands, and extending off shore from points of land. At the outlet of brooks and streams, large sand and gravel deltas often form resulting in shallows that can extend hundreds of feet off shore. Though projects for their removal are underway, these deltas are a particular problem in Lake George largely due to modern development and highway run-off.

Also pay attention to water color. Deeper water will generally appear darker blue in color. Shallows or shoals will usually appear lighter blue or even brownish in appearance. Breaking waves are also a possible indication of submerged hazards.

Charts and Maps

The first detailed nautical chart produced for Lake George was by S.R. Stoddard in 1907. Although dated, Stoddard's *Chart of Lake George* is a detailed survey of the lake providing depths, bottom types, shoreline features, hazards, and a wealth of other information. These charts are rare and difficult to find.

Since 1949, the Lake George Power Squadron has been producing the *Chart of Lake George*. This nautical chart details every aspect of navigation on Lake George including lake depths, shoreline features, navigational hazards and marker locations, and other important information for navigating on the lake. The Power Squadron's charts are available at various locations along the lake. Visit the Power Squadron's website at: www.lgps.org. Another chart (not generally available) is the "Lake George 1970 Base Chart, Prepared for State of New York Department of Conservation by Dickerson, Czerwinski, and Marneck."

Several general boaters maps for Lake George are also available. The Lake George Park Commission, in cooperation with Jimapco, Inc. have produced the *Lake George Boaters Map*, providing general boating information on the lake.

The Lake George Park Commission and Warren County Tourism Department also produce the *Lake George Fishing and Boating Map*. This map provides depth soundings for the lake, general navigational information, Island locations, and general lake regulations. This map is free, and provided when you purchase your Lake George Boat Registration.

The NY State Department of Environmental Conservation, Division of Fish, Wildlife and Marine Resources, produces the *NY Lake Map Contour Series*, providing information on depth contours, lake surface area, and fish species found in the lake. These contour maps, in two parts, are available online at: www.dec.ny.gov/docs/fish_marine_pdf.

USGS Topographic Maps (1:24,000 scale) of Lake George are available from several sources online including the USGS National Map Viewer found at: viewer.nationalmap.gov.

For an historical perspective of Lake George, S. R. Stoddard's 1897 *Map of Lake George* was reprinted in 1985, and is available for purchase at many locations along the lake. Although over 100 years old, Stoddard's map still provides a wealth of detailed information on Lake George.

Aerial imagery of Lake George can be found at Google Earth, and for download at the NY State GIS Clearinghouse website: www.nysgis.state. ny.us/gateway/mg/.

Buoyage System

Markers on Lake George are placed in accordance with the Uniform State Waterway Marking System (USWMS). This system employs two types of buoys — channel markers and regulatory markers. In critical or especially hazardous locations, these buoys may be lighted.

To understand the buoyage system, one must understand the concept of "head of navigation." On an inland body of water, the head of navigation is the source of a river, or the inlet of a lake. Although Lake George has no major inlets, its head of navigation is considered the lake's south end, since the lake discharges at its north end at Ticonderoga. When proceeding toward the head of navigation, you are said to be "returning."

Three basic types of buoys are employed on Lake George. **Can buoys** are cylindrical in shape, and can be used for regulatory markers to mark the port, or left hand side of a channel, or occasionally for mooring buoys (though most mooring buoys are spherical).

Nun Buoys are conical in shape and are used to mark the starboard, or right side of a channel. Nun buoys may also be lighted.

Spar Buoys are slender buoys that are cylindrical to indicate speed zones, or tapered with a rounded top for danger zones. They are generally smaller than cans and nuns, and can be used in place of regulatory or channel markers. The color of the spar buoy determines its function. Spar buoys are not lighted.

Lighting of buoys is based on the buoy's function. Channel markers are lighted green or red, with white lights used on regulatory markers and mooring buoys. White lights on mooring buoys are steady light so as not to be confused with regulatory buoys. Flashing lights are found on regulatory and/or channel markers. Quick flashing white lights (>50 flashes per minute) are typically reserved for buoys marking particularly dangerous shoals or other hazards. Red and green channel lights may be solid or flashing.

Channel markers are used when safe passage through a particular area can only be accomplished by following a specific route. Red and green buoys marking the channel are often placed in pairs, though they may also be staggered due to existing conditions. When navigating a channel, red, even numbered nun buoys will mark the starboard (right) side of the channel when proceeding toward the head of navigation (returning), or in the case of Lake George, **to the south**. Green, odd numbered buoys will mark the port (left) side of the channel. A classic memory aid for this is "Red, Right, Returning." When pro-

Sailboats at the Lake George Club. Photo courtesy Carl Heilman II

ceeding through a channel, favor the right side of the channel, particularly in the presence of oncoming traffic. Do not pass too closely to channel markers, however, as their position may not be precise due to drift or current.

Regulatory Markers are buoys that mark local hazards to navigation, or provide information on rules or regulations relating to a specific area. These markers consist of white cans and/or spars with orange symbols. There are four types regulatory buoys used on Lake George.

A **diamond** shape indicates *danger*. This marker may indicate a shoal, rock, log, wreck, or other hazard to navigation. This marker may be alone indicating an isolated hazard, or it may be grouped with other danger buoys or spars indicating a large obstruction. NEVER pass between grouped hazard markers. Also, never pass between a hazard buoy and the shore, if the marker is located near shore. As with any navigation buoy, its location may not be precise, so give it a wide berth.

A diamond shape with a cross indicates a vessel exclusion area. Quite frequently, these exclusion areas indicate swimming areas, close proximity to dams, or any other area where there is a danger to the vessel's crew, or others in the vicinity.

An orange circle indicates **Regulation** or **Control** markers. Common examples are no wake zones, or speed zones where the speed limit is marked within the circle. Failure to comply with regulatory markers is illegal and can result in a fine.

Informational markers are buoys with a square symbol, and offer directions, distances, or other boater information. These buoys have no navigational significance.

It is illegal to tie off or moor to a navigational buoy except in times of emergency.

Regulatory Marker Graphics

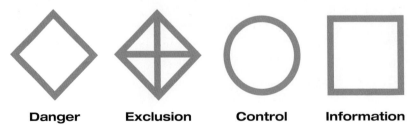

| Danger | Exclusion | Control | Information |

Lake George Boating Regulations

All boats on Lake George are subject to New York State navigation law. In addition, there are laws and regulations specific to Lake George that have been implemented for the safety of the lake's boaters, as well as to protect the quality of the lake. It is important to become familiar with these regulations, as they are strictly enforced by the lake's law enforcement agencies.

Lake George Boat Registration and Fees

Any vessel 18 feet or longer, or any vessel with a 10 HP or larger engine, must register with the Lake George Park Commission and display a user fee decal.

Boats may be registered annually, by the day, or by the week. See pages 205–206 for vendor locations on Lake George.

Temporary Boat Registrations

• **One day registration: $7.50** regardless of size or type of boat. Expires at midnight the next day following the effective date.
• **One week registration: $11.25** regardless of size or boat. Expires at midnight, seven days following effective date.

Persons berthing, operating, or using a vessel on Lake George for 21 consecutive days or more must purchase annual registrations. Any temporary registration fees paid that year may be applied toward the annual registration fee. Conversion from temporary to annual registrations must be done in person or by mail.

Calculating Your Annual Boat Fee

• Does your boat have overnight accommodations, such as bed, bunk, or sanitary facilities?
• What is your boat length? This is measured as overall length from the furthest point on the bow to the aftermost point on the stern, excluding bow pulpits, swim decks, etc. Overall length can be found on your State registration. For boats longer than 25 feet, you must round up to the next full foot.

Annual Boat Fee Schedule 2015		
Length	Equipped for Overnight	Not Equipped for Overnight
Less than 21'	$30	$30
21' to 25'	$37.50	$37.50
26'	$67.50	$45
27'	$97.50	$52.50
28'	$127.50	$60
Over 28'	$37.50 plus $30 for each foot over 25	$37.50 plus $7.50 for each foot over 25

Source: Lake George Park Commission

Protection of Lake George Water Quality

Lake George is drinking water, with many local residents taking their water from the lake. To protect the waters of Lake George several regulations are in place.

- **It is unlawful to launch a boat in Lake George without official inspection and removal of invasive species.**
- It is unlawful to discharge, dump, or throw trash or other harmful substances into the lake.
- If your vessel is equipped with a sanitary device, overboard discharge valves must be permanently disabled to prevent accidental discharge. Pump out stations are available at various locations on the lake. See pages 212–217 for a complete listing.
- The use of soaps or detergents for bathing, washing dishes, etc. is prohibited, this includes biodegradable bilge cleaners.
- **Boats painted with anti-fouling paint containing TBT (Tributylin) are not allowed on Lake George,** unless a registered Commercial Pesticides Applicator applied the paint in New York State. See NYS DEC website for more details at: www.dec.ny.gov.

Aquatic Invasive Species

Aquatic Invasive Species (AIS) are non-native plants and animals that threaten native plants, wildlife, and their habitat. They also affect humans by degrading boating and fishing areas and reducing lake shore property values and tourism. Once AIS are established, eradication is almost impossible and management programs are very expensive. Spread prevention is the most cost-effective option for protecting Lake George and other lakes across the region and New York.

Lake George currently has five known AIS: **Eurasian watermilfoil, curly-leaf pondweed, zebra mussels, Asian clam,** and **spiny water flea.** There are many more AIS that have already invaded other waterbodies close by, such as **alewife, quagga mussels** and **hydrilla.** Boats travel between these waterbodies and Lake George, creating pathways for AIS to spread.

AIS Spread Prevention

Not all hitchhikers are as visible as a boat prop covered in adult zebra mussels. Some adult or juvenile stage AIS are so small they can't be seen without magnification. Invasive viruses, zooplankton, and recently hatched zebra mussels and Asian clams can be transported in mud, on plant fragments, or in small amounts of water. When you exit a waterbody, check for anything visible while at the launch and remove it. Then wash and dry your boat and equipment more thoroughly at a boat wash station, car wash, or back home.

The Lake George Park Commission as well as all three counties bordering the lake have invasive species transport laws to help protect Lake George from the spread of AIS. Fines and other penalties vary.

Prohibited actions include:

- Launching a boat into a waterbody with any visible plants or animals attached to the boat, trailer, or other equipment.
- Entering a public highway with any visible plants or animals attached to the boat, trailer, or other equipment.
- Introducing an aquatic invasive species to any waterbody by any other means.

The Lake George Association's Lake Steward Program operates at various boat launch locations around the lake during the summer. The Lake Stewards are on hand to educate boaters about AIS spread prevention, to inspect boats and remove any hitchhikers they find, and also to collect data that is used to inform AIS spread prevention efforts. If you are at a launch with a Lake Steward, please give them a few minutes of your time to talk with them and answer their questions. To learn more about this program, you can go online to www.lakegeorgeassociation.org. You can help protect Lake George from AIS by following these guidelines:

- Clean and remove all visible plants, animals and mud from your boat, trailer, or other equipment and dispose of in a suitable trash container or on dry land before leaving the launch.
- Don't transport any potential hitchhiker, even back to your home. Remove and leave them at the site you visited.
- Drain water from bilge, live wells, ballast tanks, and any other locations with water before leaving the launch. Invasive viruses, zooplankton, and juvenile zebra mussels and Asian clams can be transported in even just a drop of water!
- Dry your boat, trailer, and all equipment completely when moving between waters to kill small species not easily seen. Drying times vary depending on the weather and the type of material. At least five days of drying time is recommended during the summer. If you want to use your boat sooner, follow additional steps to make sure it is decontaminated from any hitchhikers. Go online to www.ProtectLakeGeorge.com to find out how.

To learn more about invasive species and Lake George go to www.ProtectLakeGeorge.com.

This website has info about current AIS management efforts for to address several invasives currently found in the lake, detailed information about how to Clean, Drain, and Dry your boat, and the latest up-to-date information about the Lake George Park Commission's Invasive Species Prevention Plan, including a Mandatory Boat Inspection Program , to better protect Lake George from the introduction of additional AIS.

Launching

New Rules

As part of a multi-agency effort to combat serious invasive species threats to Lake George, new regulations for all trailered boats were put in place in 2014. **Before you launch, your boat MUST be inspected (and washed, if necessary) at one of six inspection stations located around the lake.** There is no charge for this service. Your boat will receive a tag, which will then be removed at a launch site of your choosing anywhere on the lake.

The six regional inspection stations are:

- Lake George Inspection Station: Transfer Road, Lake George
- Norowal Marina: 21 Sagamore Road, Bolton Landing
- Roger's Rock Public Campground and Boat Launch: 9894 Lakeshore Drive, Hague
- Mossy Point Public Boat Launch: Black Point Road, Ticonderoga
- Huletts Landing Marina: 6068 Lakeside Way, Huletts Landing
- Dunham's Bay Dock and Launch: 2036 Bay Road, Queensbury

For full information, clear, step-by-step instructions, and a map, go to www.lgboatinspections.com/or contact the Commission at (518) 668-9347.

Boat Launches

Several public and commercial boat launches are located on Lake George. In addition, many of the resorts, hotels, and other lodging options have boat launches. Inquire when making your reservations.

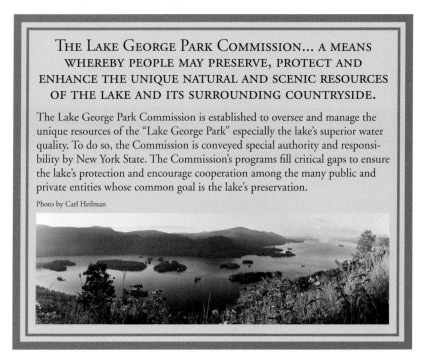

THE LAKE GEORGE PARK COMMISSION... A MEANS WHEREBY PEOPLE MAY PRESERVE, PROTECT AND ENHANCE THE UNIQUE NATURAL AND SCENIC RESOURCES OF THE LAKE AND ITS SURROUNDING COUNTRYSIDE.

The Lake George Park Commission is established to oversee and manage the unique resources of the "Lake George Park" especially the lake's superior water quality. To do so, the Commission is conveyed special authority and responsibility by New York State. The Commission's programs fill critical gaps to ensure the lake's protection and encourage cooperation among the many public and private entities whose common goal is the lake's preservation.

Photo by Carl Heilman

MANDATORY INSPECTION STATIONS

Town	Location
Lake George	Lake George Inspection Station, Transfer Road
Bolton Landing	Norowal Marina, 21 Sagamore Road
Hague	Rogers Rock Campground, 9894 Lakeshore Drive
Ticonderoga	Mossy Point Public Boat Launch, Black Point Road
Queensbury	Dunham's Bay Marina, 2036 Bay Road
Huletts Landing	Huletts Landing Marina, 6068 Lakeside Way

Launch Sites — East Side of Lake George

Million Dollar Beach	Beach Road, Lake George	668-3352
Dunham's Bay Marina	2036 Bay Rd, Queensbury	744-2647
Castaway Marina	2546 Route 9L, Queensbury	656-3636
Lake George Boat Co.	56 Boathouse Rd, Lake George	656-9203
Boats By George	291 Cleverdale Rd, Cleverdale	656-9353
Fischer's Marina	1215 Pilot Knob Rd, Kattskill Bay	656-9981
Huletts Landing Marina	6068 Lakeside Way, Huletts Landing	499-9949

Launch Sites — West Side of Lake George

Gilchrist Marina	3686 Lake Shore Dr, Diamond Point	668-5848
Yankee Marine Center	3910 Lake Shore Dr, Diamond Point	668-5696
Beckley's Boats	3950 Lake Shore Dr, Diamond Point	668-2651
Bayview Marina	4762 Lake Shore Dr, Bolton Landing	644-9633
Norowal Marina	21 Sagamore Rd, Bolton Landing	644-3741
Hague Town Beach Park	9060 Lake Shore Dr, Hague	543-6161
Rogers Rock	9894 Lake Shore Dr, Hague	644-3831
Mossy Point	Black Point Rd, Ticonderoga	897-1310

Anchoring, Docking, and Mooring

One of the most enjoyable aspects of boating on Lake George is spending an afternoon on the "hook" relaxing, grilling, swimming, or just taking in the extraordinary beauty of the lake. Countless locations suitable for anchoring can be found on the lake, and with a little exploration you just might find your "one particular harbor." While not a difficult procedure, being familiar with a few anchoring basics will make your time at anchor more enjoyable and safe. Follow these basic steps:

1. Choose your anchorage with several factors in mind including wind direction, lake conditions, bottom type, depth, local boat traffic, and proximity of anchored boats. Find a location offering protection from the wind and waves. Check your chart for bottom type: mud, clay, or sandy-mud provides the best holding. Avoid anchoring in rocky or weedy areas, since the holding will be poor, or worse, your anchor may become fouled. Avoid anchoring in excessively deep water: 10–30 feet of water is usually best. The ideal scope (anchor line) for anchoring is a **ratio of 6:1**, or in other words, 60 feet of anchor line for every 10 feet of water. In heavier winds and seas you may want to pay out as much as a 10:1 scope. Also be sure that you leave enough "swing" room between you and nearby anchored boats. And finally, be sure the bitter end of your anchor line is secured to the boat. While that may seem obvious, over my many years diving in Lake George, I have found numerous lost anchors complete with 40 or 50 feet of anchor line attached.

2. When ready to drop anchor, make your approach slowly and into the wind. When you reach the spot where you wish the anchor to lay, take all headway off the boat. When your forward motion has stopped, have your crew lower (not throw) the anchor to the bottom.

3. Slowly back away from the anchor, being careful to pay out the anchor line slowly to avoid fouling your prop.

4. When about a 4:1 scope has been let out, snub the anchor line to a bow cleat, and gently throttle up in reverse to set the anchor. The anchor line should tighten and the boat should stop moving aft. If you feel the line "chatter" or skip, go to neutral, let out more anchor line, and repeat the process until the

anchor is set. You will know the anchor is set when the boat springs forward after going from reverse to neutral. Be extremely careful during this process that your crew's body or fingers do not get between the boat and the anchor line. If you cannot get the anchor to set, haul it up, and try another location. Don't be embarrassed; there is not a skipper out there who has not had to make multiple attempts at anchoring.

5. Confirm you are securely anchored and check your swing. Spend a few minutes observing how your boat drifts at anchor in relation to nearby boats. Also, line up two points on land. If their alignment changes, you may be dragging anchor. If so, let out more scope if possible. If conditions allow, the most reliable method to check that the anchor is properly set is to put on your mask and fins and check it visually.

6. To weigh (haul in) anchor, simply reverse the process.

There are several regulations for anchoring on Lake George.

• **Anchoring within 200 feet offshore from private property is prohibited.***
• Sandy Bay at the southeast end of the lake is a **restricted use zone**. Boats must use the provided moorings, which are on a first-come/first-serve basis. Anchoring, rafting, or tying off to shore in Sandy Bay is prohibited.
• Paradise Bay is also a **restricted use zone**. Anchoring, rafting, or tying off to shore is prohibited, but only between May 15 and September 15
• **Anchoring is prohibited** in the Waltonian Islands.

*Many of the local homes and resorts draw drinking water from intake piping extending into the lake. Fouling of these intake pipes with your anchor could cause severe damage to their water systems, and result in a hefty bill if you are found responsible. Respect the 200-foot regulation.

Docking

Countless variables are involved when docking and undocking including wind, seas, current, boat type, size, etc. Consequently, there is no single set of rules that can guide every boat operator in every situation. However, by following several precautions, knowing your boat's handling characteristics, and using common sense, docking is safe and easy.

Several tips for safe docking and undocking

1. Make preparations for docking, such as setting dock lines, fenders, etc., well in advance.

2. Be sure all passengers keep their hands inboard.

3. When making your approach to the dock, slow to bare steerageway, and watch for swimmers, kayakers, etc.

4. Adjust for wind and/or current (approach the upwind side of the dock if possible).

5. Remember that a boat's stern will pivot around the bow.

When undocking

1. Keep hands clear of pylons and dock.

2. Be sure to bring all dock lines inboard and stow them. (One of the more common sources of expensive power train damage is dock lines fouling props).

3. Take your time leaving the dock. You are responsible for your wake, and you can be held responsible for any damage caused to nearby boats or property.

Mooring

Mooring buoys are commonly white spherical buoys with blue bands. The key to picking up a mooring buoy is preparation, and taking your time. With a crew member on the bow standing by with boat hook in hand, approach the mooring buoy from downwind. Keep just enough speed on the boat for steerageway. When your bow reaches the mooring, go to neutral and have your crew bring the mooring pendant aboard with the boat hook and secure it to the bow cleat. Keep the engine running until your crew gives word that the pendant is securely made to the cleat. If you overshoot the mooring buoy, use just enough reverse to check your forward motion. If you miss the buoy, go around for another

A mooring buoy. Photo by Scott Padeni

attempt. Be extremely careful not to foul the prop in the mooring pendant. Go to neutral and let the wind carry you off if necessary.

When leaving a mooring buoy, the wind should already have you positioned downwind of the buoy. Start your engine, leave it in neutral, and drop the mooring buoy pendant. When the boat drifts downwind a few boat lengths, slowly pull away staying well clear of the mooring buoy pendant, to avoid fouling your prop. If there is no wind, put the boat in reverse and slowly back away from the mooring buoy pendant.

Speed Limits

Speed Limits on Lake George are limited to a maximum of:
• 45 mph between 6:00 am and 9:00 pm
• 25 mph between 9:00 pm and 6:00 am
• 5 mph within 100 feet of docks, moorings, anchored vessels, and no wake zones.
• Remember, you are responsible for your own wake. Be aware of how your wake will affect those around you.

Noise Limits

Because of the narrow, mountainous nature of Lake George, sound from powerboats can be problematic. Lake George sound limits for powerboats are 86 decibels when measured not more than 50 feet from the vessel; 80 decibels from 100 feet or more. These noise limits are strictly enforced. Contact the Lake George Park Commission in advance if you have doubts as to your vessel's compliance.

Safety Equipment

Boats on Lake George are subject to the minimum safety standards as set by the United States Coast Guard (USCG).

It is your responsibility to be sure your vessel meets these requirements. Your boat manufacturer meets many of the USCG safety requirements. Others include (see next page):

- You must have at least one U.S.C.G. approved **personal flotation device** (PFD) for each person on board. Each PFD must be in serviceable condition.
- PFDs must be the appropriate size for the intended wearer.
- Type V PFDs, such as inflatable vests or belts, must be worn to count as a PFD.
- Vessels less than 26 feet in length must carry at least one Type IV PFD, such as a throw cushion or ring buoy (manually powered craft less than 16 feet are exempt).
- Vessels larger than 26 feet but less than 65 must carry at least two ring buoys.
- PFDs must be stowed in an accessible location, not in the plastic bags in which they were originally purchased.
- Children under 12 years of age must wear PFDs at all times.
- Each person in a vessel less than 21 feet in length, including canoes, kayaks, and other manually propelled water craft, must wear a PFD at all times between November 1 and May 1.
- Power driven vessels must have a type B-1 fire extinguisher, whistle or horn audible at least a half mile, anchor and rode, distress flag, and flares (check expiration date). Vessels greater than 26 feet must have two B-1 fire extinguishers or one type B-2.
- Gasoline powered vessels with inboard or inboard/outboard engines must have carburetor flame arrestors.

For the complete New York Navigation Law and required equipment go to: www.nyss.com/NYS.html#p40.

Waterskiing and Tubing

Anyone water skiing, tubing, or otherwise being towed behind a boat must wear a Type III PFD. An observer must also be in the towboat, independent of the boat operator, and be at least 10 years of age.

Personal Watercraft (PWC)

In addition to applicable New York State Law, Lake George has unique regulations regarding Personal Watercraft (PWCs). Just like powerboats, PWCs are considered motor vehicles, and regulations pertaining to their operation are strictly enforced. Familiarizing yourself with these regulations in advance will make your time on the lake much more enjoyable.

• PWCs can only be operated between 8 am and 7 pm.

• The speed limit for PWCs is 5 mph within 500 feet of shore.

• PWCs cannot be operated within 500 feet of a designated swimming area or mooring field.

• Operators of PWCs must be at least 14 years of age.

• A mandatory NY State safety certificate is required for PWC operators, regardless of age, and must be carried at all times when operating.

• Persons over the age of 18 renting PWCs may operate them without having to hold a boating safety certificate if under the supervision of the rental agent.

Communications

VHF

For emergencies, Lake George marine patrols and other emergency personnel monitor VHF radio Channel-16. For general communication, commercial vessels, most marinas, Tow U.S., and many of the waterfront businesses also monitor VHF. Weather reports broadcast by NOAA and from the U.S.C.G. station at Burlington, Vt. can also be received on VHF on Lake George.

9-1-1

Emergencies can also be reported using 911 on your cell phone. In many areas of the lake, particularly in the Narrows, cell phone coverage can be spotty.

Emergency Contact Information

Lake George Park Commission Marine Patrol	(518) 668-9347
New York State Police Marine Patrol	(518) 644-2555
Bolton Police	(518) 644-9717
Lake George Sheriff	(518) 743-2500
(Emergency)	(518) 761-6477
Washington County Emergency Service	(518) 747-7520
Ambulance Squad	911
Fire Departments	911
Glens Falls Hospital	(518) 926-1000

Ranger Stations

Ranger Stations are available to assist boaters at several locations on the Lake.

• The southernmost Ranger Station is on Long Island (518-656-9426).
• The Glen Island Ranger Station (518-644-9696) is located on Glen Island in the Narrows.
• The Narrow Island Ranger Station (518-499-1288) is located on Narrow Island just west of Huletts Landing.

Float Plan

It is advisable that before setting out on the lake, you let someone on shore or at home know of your plans. Whether in a powerboat, kayak, or paddleboat, leave a note at the lobby desk, on your kitchen table, or wherever family or friends are likely to find it. For short jaunts on the lake, give them the basic details of where you plan to go, and how long you'll be away. For longer excursions, detail the places you plan to visit, how long you plan to be at each, and what time you expect to return. You may also want to include emergency contact numbers, just in case. "Better safe than sorry" is a good rule to follow.

Sun Exposure and Hypothermia

There's nothing more enjoyable than basking in the sun on a beautiful Lake George day. But remember to practice moderation and drink plenty of water, for too much sun can lead to sunburn, dehydration, heat exhaustion, and even life-threatening heat stroke.

Don't let too much sun ruin your vacation!

One of the greatest hazards posed to boaters on Lake George is **hypothermia**. Lake George is a spring fed lake, and as such can remain cold well into the summer. In spring and even into June, it is not uncommon to enjoy 80-degree air temperatures, with water temperatures not rising above 60 degrees. This can be a dangerous combination for unsuspecting swimmers, or for boaters suffering a capsize, since water that cold can pose a serious threat. Exposure to water temperatures of 60 degrees can lead to incapacity or unconsciousness in less than two hours. The amount of time before unconsciousness occurs decreases with a decrease in water temperature. Though less rapid, hypothermia can also occur in water as warm as 80 degrees. Despite what old wives' tales may suggest, alcohol should not be given to anyone suffering from hypothermia as it only increases the loss of body heat.

Three stages of hypothermia

- **Stage I Hypothermia** — Just about everyone has experienced this as a child at the beach. It is characterized by feeling cold, goose bumps, violent shivering, and slurred speech. Stage I hypothermia is treated by removing the victim from the water, wrapping them in a towel or blanket, and giving them warm fluids (NO ALCOHOL).
- **Stage II Hypothermia** — Symptoms include incoherence, drowsiness, exhaustion, and loss of muscular control. Grasping a lifeline can be difficult. Ears, lips, fingertips, and toes may appear bluish. Stage II hypothermia cannot be treated by simply wrapping the victim in a blanket; an external heat source is required. On a boat, a shared blanket with a crewmember can supply body heat until the victim can get indoors, or medical attention arrives.
- **Stage III Hypothermia** — This is the most severe, and is characterized by collapse and unconsciousness, respiratory distress, and/or possible cardiac arrest. This stage of hypothermia is a medical emergency and requires immediate medical assistance.

Drinking and Boating (BUI)

A common misconception by some boaters on Lake George is that it's OK to drink while enjoying a day of boating on the lake. As with driving a car intoxicated, drinking while operating a boat is illegal and will be dealt with harshly by local law enforcement agencies.

Be safe — boat sober!!

Boating "Rules of the Road"

As with driving your vehicle, there is an established set of "Rules of the Road" for vessels on the water. Properly termed "Navigation Rules," they are designed to provide guidance to boat operators by setting a standard of actions that should be followed by boaters in order to prevent collisions. These rules are written in terms of "vessel," which includes watercraft of all sizes, from jet skis to the largest cabin cruisers. **ALL vessels must adhere to these rules**; therefore an understanding of the rules by boat operators is critical. No one is excused if they fail to comply, and may be held legally accountable if found negligent.

Several meeting situations are covered by the rules, using the terms "Give-Way" and "Stand-On" to describe the vessels involved. In meeting situations between two boats, the stand-on vessel is generally required to maintain course and speed. The give-way vessel is required to take early and substantial action in order to avoid collision. Unfortunately, not all boaters are familiar with the "Navigation Rules," so if a give-way vessel fails to yield, **be prepared to take evasive action even though you are entitled to the right of way.** A detailed discussion of the 38 Navigation Rules is beyond the scope of this boater's guide; however listed on the following pages are the situations most commonly encountered by boaters. It is highly recommended that every boat operator have a copy of the U.S.C.G Navigation Rules on board at all times.

Meeting Head-On

When two power-driven vessels meet on reciprocal or nearly reciprocal headings, each vessel is required to exchange a short blast of their horn and pass with each other on their port (left) side. At night, you will know that you are in a head-on situation when you see both red and green sidelights of the oncoming vessel.

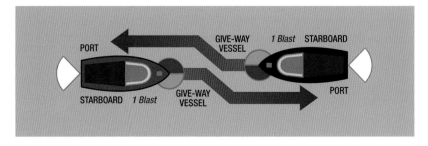

Crossing Situation

This is a situation in which two power-driven vessels are crossing and risk of collision exists. In this situation, the vessel that has the other on its starboard side is the give-way vessel. The give-way vessel should sound one blast on its horn, turn to starboard, and leave the stand-on vessel on its port side. The stand-on vessel should respond with one short blast and maintain course and speed. If either vessel fails to take the proper action, the other vessel should give the 5-blast danger-doubt signal, and back down until the second vessels takes the proper action. At night in a crossing situation, the give-way vessel will see the red (port) side light of the stand-on vessel to starboard; the stand-on vessel will see the green (starboard) sidelight of the give-way vessel to port.

As memory aids, think: "port wine red" and "red means stop, green means go."

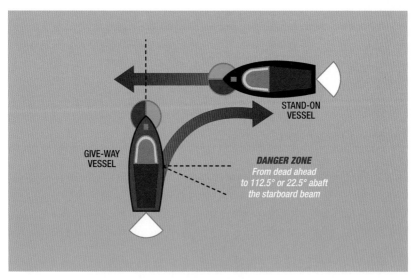

Diagrams show boats with regulation lights (red: port or left; green: starboard or right on bow; white: aft or stern).

Overtaking Situation

An overtaking situation exists when a vessel approaches another at an angle 22 ½ degrees or more "abaft," or behind, the other vessel's beam. In this situation, the overtaking vessel is deemed the give-way vessel and must keep clear of the vessel being overtaken. The vessel being overtaken is required to maintain course and speed until the give-way vessel is past and clear. The overtaking vessel will sound one (passing to starboard) or two (passing to port) blasts on their horn. If in agreement, the vessel being overtaken should respond with the same signal. If there is any doubt by either vessel as to the actions of the other, they should sound the 5-blast danger-doubt signal, and stand by until the proper response is given. Sailing vessels under sail lose their right of way when they are the overtaking vessel.

When in an overtaking situation at night, the over-taking vessel will see the white stern light of the vessel being overtaken. The vessel being overtaken, or stand-on vessel, will look astern and see both the red and green sidelights of the over-taking vessel.

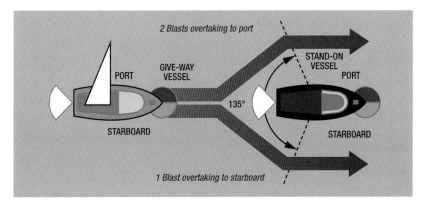

Sailing Vessels

A sailing vessel is defined as a vessel propelled by sails only. If under sail *and* power, they are considered a power-driven vessel and lose their right-of-way as a sailing vessel.

- Generally, vessels under sail have the right-of-way over power driven vessels.
- When two vessels under sail approach one another so as to involve the risk of collision:

  - The sailing vessel on the port tack (wind on the port side) shall keep out of the way of the sailing vessel on the starboard tack (wind on the starboard side).
  - When both sailing vessels are on the same tack (wind on the same side), the windward (up wind) vessel shall keep out of the way of the leeward (down wind) vessel.
  - When a sailing vessel on the port tack cannot determine if a windward (up wind) sailing vessel is on the port or starboard tack, the leeward (down wind) vessel will assume the role of give-way vessel and stay out of the way of the other.

Narrow Channel Rules

- A vessel in a narrow channel or fairway shall keep as far to the right of that channel as is safe and practical.
- A vessel less than 20 meters (66 ft.), sailing vessel, ski boat, jet ski, or manually driven vessel shall not impede the passage of a vessel that can safely operate only within that channel or fairway.
- A vessel shall not cross a narrow channel if it impedes the passage of another vessel that can safely operate only within that channel or fairway.
- Any vessel rounding an obstructed bend in a narrow channel shall sound one prolonged whistle signal, and proceed with extreme caution.
- All vessels should avoid anchoring in a narrow channel.

Navigation Lights

- Must be displayed between sunset and sunrise, or in conditions of reduced visibility, such as fog or rain.
- Rowboats, and sailboats under 7 meters (22 ft.) in length need only show a white light in sufficient time to prevent collision.
- Vessels at anchor are required to show an all-around (360°) white light when anchored in a non-designated anchorage. Vessels less than 7 meters (22 ft.) in length, not in a traffic area, are exempt from this rule.

Required Sound Signals

When risk of collision exists between vessels in sight of one another, the exchange of sound signals is required. Each of these sound signals provides indication to the other of their intent to maneuver.

- **One short blast** means: "I intend to leave you to my port side," which means you will turn to starboard.
- **Two short blasts** mean: "I intend to leave you to my starboard side," which means you will turn to port.
- **Three short blasts** mean: "I am operating in astern propulsion." This signals to others that you are operating in reverse.
- **Five or more short blasts** mean: the danger-doubt signal, used when either vessel doubts the other vessel is taking proper or sufficient action to avoid collision.

Zebra Mussel

Eurasian Watermilfoil

Water Chestnut

Alewife (6")

STATE OF NEW YORK

LAKE L G GEORGE
PARK COMMISSION

A NEW YORK STATE ENVIRONMENTAL, PLANNING AND PUBLIC SAFETY AGENCY
DEVOTED TO THE PRESERVATION OF LAKE GEORGE AND THE SAFETY OF ITS USERS.
tel: (518) 668-9347 • fax: (518) 668-5001 • e-mail: info@lgpc.state.ny.us • www.lgpc.state.ny.us

Become informed and take action! Be a part of the solution.

The Boaters Guide to Knots

Like any trade or occupation, there are specific skills that should be mastered by the conscientious boater. One of those skills is knot work, also known as marlinespike seamanship. So important is this skill to the mariner, that "old salts" will often judge the seamanship of a boat's skipper by their ability to tie a line, and rightly so. The inability to tie the proper knot for a specific job can result in damage or even loss of your boat, or worse, harm to your crew.

Marlinspike seamanship is a tradition dating back thousands of years and includes knots, line splicing, and decorative rope work. There are literally hundreds of knots to choose from; however, for the recreational boater, the ability to tie the knots described in detail below will be sufficient. There are three basic types of knots: the **hitch** is used to attach a line to a spar, rail, post, ring, cleat, or even another line; a **bend** joins two lines together; and a **knot** (somewhat confusingly) is anything not included in the hitch or bend categories, and includes stopper knots, loop knots, and binding knots.

As with knots, specific types of line are used for specific tasks. And for all of you landlubbers, remember—there are "no ropes on a boat." To the seasoned mariner, once a "rope" is onboard, it becomes a "line."

▌ Natural fibers such as hemp, sisal, cotton and manila are inexpensive, but are much weaker than synthetic fiber lines and are prone to rot.

▌ Nylon is the strongest of the manmade lines and can stretch up to 40 percent and still regain its original length. Nylon line does not float. The shock-absorbing characteristics of nylon make it ideal for mooring and dock lines, as well as towlines and anchor lines.

▌ Dacron is another synthetic line. It has 75 percent of the strength of nylon but is far less elastic. As with nylon, dacron does not float. For these reasons, dacron is ideal for the running rigging and some of the standing rigging of sailing vessels.

▌ Polypropylene is one of the most inexpensive of the manmade lines and can be ranked between natural fiber and other more expensive synthetics. It has less than one-half the breaking strength of nylon. It is also the lightest of the synthetics and will float indefinitely. These characteristics make polypropylene ideal for mooring pendants and ski lines.

Described below are several basic knots, hitches and bends that a mariner should know. In fact, these basic knots are part of the USCG exams for those seeking a commercial captain's license.

The Bowline

The bowline (pronounced "boh-linn") is a loop knot and is arguably the most useful knot to the boater. This knot results in a loop that can be used for a multitude of tasks, ranging from securing the corner of a sail, to serving as a life-saving "sling" with which to recover a man overboard. The bowline has several advantages in that it will not slip or loosen, and can be untied even after the heaviest of loads have been placed upon it.

1. Form an overhand loop in the standing line.
2. Pass the working end (bitter end) of the line up through the loop.
3. Pass the working end around the back of the standing line then back down through the loop.
4. Tighten the knot. An age-old method of remembering how to tie this knot is: "The rabbit comes up through the hole, around the back of the tree (in this case the standing line), and then back down the hole."

Square Knot (Reef Knot)

The square, or reef knot dates back to the time of the ancient Romans and is used to bind two ends of the same line. The name reef knot comes from its being used to bind sails being "reefed" or shortened during a building wind.

1. Make a loop at one end of the line.
2. Pass the other end of the same line up through the loop then around the loop's backside.
3. Now pass the end back down through the loop and tighten.

The square or reef knot is often confused with its close cousin, the granny knot.

Clove Hitch

The clove hitch is used to secure a dock line to a post or pylon. A single clove hitch is prone to inadvertent release in rough conditions, so the use of a series of clove hitches is recommended when docking.

1. Form an overhand loop at a convenient point in the dock line.
2. Add an underhand loop a short length down the line so the pair looks like two opposing "Mickey Mouse" ears.
3. Overlap the two loops.
4. Place the overlapped loops over the spar, dock post or pylon you are securing your boat to then tighten. Repeat this process for additional clove hitches.

Clove hitch, continued

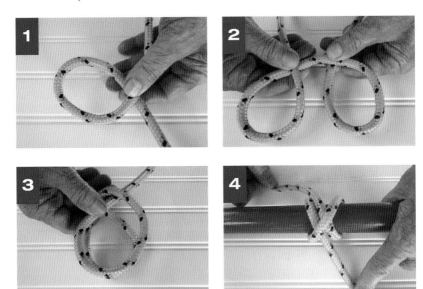

Round Turns and Half Hitches

This extremely simple and strong hitch is similar to the clove hitch as it can be used to secure a boat to a dock, or to secure cargo.

1. Make two turns around the ring or dock post.
2. Bring the working end back to itself and make a half hitch.
3. Make a second half hitch.
4. Tighten the half hitches. (For a more secure hitch, whip the working end of the line to itself).

See round turnand half hitch photos 3 and 4 on next page.

Round turn and half hitch, continued

Sheet Bend (Becket Bend) and Double Sheet Bend

The sheet bend or becket bend, and its variant the double becket bend are also ancient knots used by mariners for thousands of years. They were, and still are, used to fasten the loop on a corner of a sail, called a becket, to the "sheet," or the line used to control the corner of a sail when underway. They are also used to fasten two lines of different size and stiffness.

1. Create a "becket" at the end of one of the lines being tied.
2. Take the second line and feed it up through the becket.
3. Run the working end beneath the becket.
4. Tuck the working end under itself and tighten.
5. For the double sheet bend, simply make a second turn of the working end around the becket.

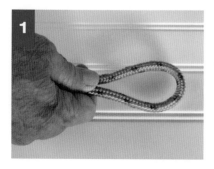 

Sheet bend and double sheet bend, continued

 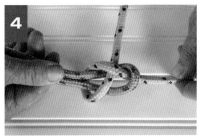

Anchor Bend (Fisherman's Bend)

This bend has been used for centuries by fisherman securing wet and slippery line to an anchor ring. This knot is extremely strong, chafe resistant, and when combined with a whipping will prevent the accidental loss of your anchor.

1. Pass the working end of the line through the anchor ring or shackle.
2. Pass the working end of the line through the anchor ring or shackle a second time.
3. Pass the working end through the two loops just created.
4. Bring the working end back to the line and tie two half hitches.
5. For added security, leave extra length on the working end and whip it to the main body of the anchor line with synthetic twine.

See photos 1 through 5 on next page.

Anchor bend, continued

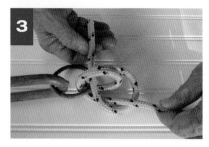
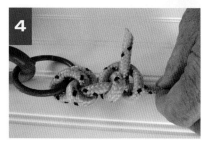

Common Whipping

Electrical tape is quite often the means by which your average boater prevents the "bitter end" of a line from fraying. The "old salt" on the other hand, would shudder at such a thought. For he knows that the only proper method of finishing the working end of a line is by whipping it. Whippings are used to prevent the fraying of a line's "bitter end," and as mentioned above, or to prevent more permanent knots such as anchor bends from coming untied.

1. Make a loop with your whipping twine and hold it and the bitter end of the line with one hand.

2. Beginning approximately one inch from the end of the line, tightly wind the whipping twine around the line and twine loop, working your way back toward the line's end.

3. When you reach the loop in the whipping twine, pass the working end of the twine through the loop.

4. Now pull the other end of the whipping twine. This draws in the loop and cinches the whip. Finally, cut away the two working ends of the whipping twine.

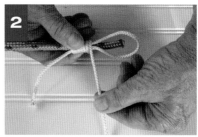

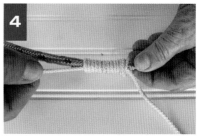

For more information on knots and marlinespike seamanship, see *The Ashley Book of Knots*, by Clifford W. Ashley (Doubleday 1944); and *The Ultimate Encyclopedia of Knots and Ropework*, by Geoffrey Budworth (Anness Publishing Ltd, 1999). An excellent online source is *Animated Knots* By Grog (www.animatedknots.com). This website provides step-by-step animations for tying just about any knot imaginable.

Other boating activities: Scuba Diving & Snorkeling, Fishing, Sailing, Kayaking, and Paddleboarding

Scuba Diving and Snorkeling

Whether you are an advanced or novice diver, the crystal clear waters, unique geology, and historic shipwrecks of Lake George make it an ideal diving destination. Because of the clear waters of the lake, depths can be deceiving, so watch your gauges. As always, plan your dive — dive your plan.

Regulations

Several regulations are in place to protect scuba divers and boaters, as well as the lake's heritage:

• Scuba diving is prohibited in navigable channels and where it would interfere with free and safe access to docks and boathouses.
• Dive flags are required. Boats must stay at least 100 feet away from dive flags.
• Removal of historic artifacts from the bottom of Lake George is illegal.

Local and Regional Dive Shops

Three dive shops are available in the general vicinity of Lake George:

• **Halfmoon Marine Services (518) 357-3234**
Based out of Gilchrist Marina, Bolton. Offering dive and specialty charters.

• **Rich Morin's Professional Scuba Centers (518) 761-0533**
20 Warren Street, Glens Falls, NY 12801 (approximately 10 miles south of Lake George Village) Offering dive charters, equipment, and lessons.

• **Seguin's Scuba Center (518) 456-8146**
1592 Central Avenue, Albany, NY 12205 (approximately 55 miles south of Lake George Village) Offering dive charters on Lake George, gear rental and sales, and scuba courses.

Submerged Heritage Preserves:
An Underwater State Park for Scuba Divers
by Joseph W. Zarzynski, RPA (Bateaux Below, Inc.)

In September 1993, the State of New York and several non-government organizations opened the first shipwreck preserves for visiting scuba enthusiasts in the Empire State. Called "Submerged Heritage Preserves," the underwater park is administered by the New York State Dept. of Environmental Conservation (DEC). Bateaux Below, Inc., a not-for-profit corporation that studies shipwrecks in Lake George, has a Memorandum of Understanding with the DEC to help set up, monitor, and break down the seasonal scuba park.

This unique state park provides "controlled public access" for scuba divers to three shipwreck preserves: "The Sunken Fleet of 1758," "The *Forward* Underwater Classroom," and "*Land Tortoise:* A 1758 Floating Gun Battery." A set of two buoys, a blue-and-white mooring buoy and an orange-and-white navigational aid buoy, mark each preserve site. Underwater trail lines guide divers around each shipwreck preserve. A DEC-produced brochure is available on the Internet (www. dec.ny.gov/lands/315.html) to provide divers with a history of each shipwreck preserve, regulations, location of each site, details on mooring procedures, emergency information, and even a suggested reading list to find out more about these historic shipwrecks.

"The Sunken Fleet of 1758" and "The *Forward* Underwater Classroom" preserves are open from Memorial Day Weekend in late May into the early autumn. These can be visited on a first-come, first-served basis. "*Land Tortoise:* A 1758 Floating Gun Battery" is open the second Saturday in June through Labor Day in September. Due to the depth of the *Land Tortoise* radeau, a one-of-a-kind colonial vessel lying in 105–107 ft. of water, and because of its historical significance, this shipwreck preserve is dived by registration only. Divers must first get a registration permit from the DEC office at Million Dollar Beach before diving the radeau; see the web site for more information.

To protect these shipwrecks and the preserves' underwater trail lines and signage, there is no anchoring within 500 ft. of preserves' buoys. Dive boats should use the mooring buoys to access preserve sites and only one boat at a time should be tied to each mooring buoy.

The Sunken Fleet of 1758 This site has seven 1758 British bateaux from the French and Indian War (1755–1763) and a 23 ft. long replica bateau deliberately sunk in 1997. The bateau (spelled bateaux in the plural) was the utilitarian watercraft of its time. They were generally 25–40 ft. long, flat-bottomed, and pointed at bow and stern. An oar tied off the stern was used for steerage. They were primarily rowed, but a crude mast and sail could be employed. In shallow water they also could be poled. In 1758, the British deliberately sank part of their fleet including 260 bateaux to protect them from French raiders over the winter of 1758–1759. It is believed that over forty bateaux were not retrieved in 1759 and today they are shipwrecks. This preserve's replica bateau, built by public school students from Bolton, Minerva, and Newcomb schools, provides visiting divers with the opportunity to see what an intact bateau would look like and to test how a sunken wooden vessel undergoes "site formation processes" to become a "shipwreck." This preserve site is located on the east side of Lake George about one mile north of Million Dollar Beach. The preserve is stretched out over about 450 ft. and lies in 20–40 ft. of water. Underwater signage and trail lines guide visiting divers around the site. State law requires that divers tow a red-and-white dive flag. ***Do not touch or disturb the bateau wrecks.*** They are British shipwrecks and are protected by local, state, and federal laws. These bateaux were mapped by Bateaux Below from 1987–1991 and in 1992, the seven colonial shipwrecks, called the Wiawaka Bateaux after the nearby Wiawaka Holiday House, were listed on the National Register of Historic Places.

The Forward Underwater Classroom This preserve was originally called "The *Forward*," named after the 45 ft. long, 1906-built, early gasoline-powered motor launch named *Forward*. The site is located about 1,500 ft. east of Diamond Island. The Bixby family of Bolton Landing originally owned the *Forward*. One of the Bixby family members was a key financial supporter of Charles A. Lindbergh's 1927 trans-Atlantic flight from the USA to France. Over 1997–1998, The *Forward* preserve underwent a transformation. With state permission, a wooden cabin cruiser was sunk near the *Forward* and Bateaux Below divers installed a 500 ft. long triangular trail system. Divers tour the preserve and visit informational signage explaining about fish life, geology, vegetation, and color loss at depth. The preserve has an underwater navigation course, slates for divers to record temperature changes due to depth, a zebra mussel monitoring station, an underwater archaeology grid placed over the sunken wooden cabin cruiser, and a horizontal secchi disk to record water transparency. The preserve's hardware transformation was financed by a small grant for the Fund for Lake George, Inc. The preserve lies in 20–45 ft. of water. In November 2008, the *Forward* shipwreck was listed on the National Register of Historic Places. Visiting divers must tow a red-and-white diver flag; note the mooring is for dive boats and not fishing vessels.

Land Tortoise: A 1758 Floating Gun Battery In August 1994, the 1758 *Land Tortoise* radeau shipwreck opened as the third shipwreck preserve. The seven sided, 52 ft. long × 18 ft. wide wooden vessel was pierced for seven guns. The British deliberately sank the radeau (French for "raft")—a type of floating gun battery—on October 22, 1758 to protect it from French marauders. However, it ended up in deep water and was found by Bateaux Below on June 26, 1990 during a Klein side scan sonar survey. Bateaux Below studied this remarkably intact sunken vessel from 1991–1993, under the direction of Dr. D.K. Abbass. The *Land Tortoise* radeau, was listed on the National Register of Historic Places in 1995 and in 1998 it was designated a National Historic Landmark, only the sixth shipwreck in American waters with that historic recognition. Due to its depth, lying in 105–107 ft. of water, diving is by registration only. The dive boat should fly the red-and-white diver flag. This dive is for experienced divers only. Each diver should carry an auxiliary pony bottle scuba tank for safety. Divers are asked not to touch or damage the fragile shipwreck. Read the DEC brochure for dive protocol before diving the site. Safety is a must!

For more information and safety guidelines for diving the Lake George Underwater Heritage Preserve, go to: www.dec.ny.gov/outdoor/7830.html.

For more information on these shipwrecks consult:

Book: *Sails and Steam in the Mountains—A Maritime and Military History of Lake George and Lake Champlain* by Russell P. Bellico (Purple Mountain Press, Fleischmanns, New York, 1992); (www.catskill.net/purple/)

DVD documentary: *The Lost Radeau: North America's Oldest Intact Warship* (57 min., Pepe Productions, Glens Falls, New York, 2005); (www.thelostradeau.com)

DVD documentary: *Wooden Bones: The Sunken Fleet of 1758* (58 min., Pepe Productions & Bateaux Below, Inc., Glens Falls, New York, 2010); (www.woodenbones.com)

Fishing on Lake George

Lake George offers both novice and experienced fishermen numerous and varied fishing opportunities all around the lake. There are several species of fish in Lake George, some of which can be fished year round.

Fishing Regulations

Fishing on Lake George is under the control of the New York State Department of Environmental Conservation. Information and licensing regulations available for download can be found at their website at http://www.dec.ny.gov/outdoor/fishing.html. Additionally, special fishing regulations for Lake George can be found at www.dec.ny.gov/outdoor/89511.html. Generally:

- Under 16 years of age, no license is necessary.
- Snagging, possession, and use of smelt and alewife as bait is illegal in Lake George.
- Taking bass off nests is illegal, as is fishing out of season.
- Disregarding minimum size limits is illegal, as is exceeding maximum catch allowances.

Fishing License Fees 2015	
Resident License	**Fee**
Senior (70 years+/Military Disability	$6.00
Annual Fishing	$25.00
7-Day Fishing	$12.00
1-Day Fishing	$5.00
Non-Resident License	**Fee**
Annual Fishing	$50.00
7-Day Fishing	$28.00
1-Day Fishing	$10.00

Lake George Sport Fish Species

Bluegill & Pumpkinseed — These two members of the Sunfish Family have been combined here because they share a number of common attributes. Both fish are of similar size; both are flat, deep-bodied and colorful; both are usually found in shallow water close to shore; but most of all, both are quite easy to catch. Many a young angler got their start by snagging one of these fish with nothing more than a string with a bobber and worm.

Bluegill (NYSDEC).   Pumpkinseed (NYSDEC).

Rock Bass — This species, also a member of the Sunfish Family, is often found in groups in Lake George among the rocky and gravelly shallows of the lake. Despite reaching only ten inches in length, rock bass are popular with many anglers and have earned the nickname "redeyes" due to their bright red eyes.

Yellow Perch — Yellow perch are very adaptable, and can be found in many varied habitats throughout Lake George. Since they prefer shallow water and are easy to catch, they are often one of the first fish caught by the novice angler. This delicious pan fish is also a favorite of ice fishermen.

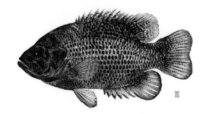

Rock Bass (NYSDEC).   Yellow Perch (NYSDEC).

88

Smallmouth Bass — Smallmouth bass are respected for the spirited fight they give an angler once hooked. They prefer lakes and streams with clear water and gravel or rocky bottoms, conditions found throughout Lake George. Since smallmouths will eat whatever live prey may be available, success can be had using a variety of both live and artificial baits

Largemouth Bass — Like their cousins the smallmouths, largemouth bass can be relied on to give a good fight. But unlike their cousins, they prefer to stay in shallow weedy areas of lakes and streams, often staying close to submerged cover such as logs and docks. Although they will also respond to a variety of live and artificial baits, enticing them from their cover is more of a challenge than fishing for most other panfish.

Smallmouth Bass (NYSDEC).　　　Largemouth Bass (NYSDEC).

Pickerel — Chain Pickerel are another favorite game fish of ice fishermen on Lake George. In the other three seasons, pickerel prefer the cover of heavy weed growth found in quieter waters. Averaging one to two pounds and fifteen to twenty inches in length, they can be very challenging to land with light tackle.

Northern Pike — Northern Pike resemble their cousins the pickerels, but can grow to a much larger size, sometimes exceeding forty pounds. Because of their size and predatory nature, northern pike play an important role in controlling overpopulation of smaller fish species. Northerns prefer the weedy areas of the lake and inlet streams, with larger adults moving into the deeper waters of the lake. This is another species that is fished year round.

Chain Pickerel (NYSDEC).　　　Northern Pike (NYSDEC).

89

Rainbow Trout— Rainbow Trout, a species native to the Pacific coast, was introduced into New York in the late nineteenth century. Similar in appearance to some salmon, rainbow trout can be quite variable in size. Only a pound or two in streams, rainbows that move into deeper lake waters can exceed ten pounds or more. Often leaping out of the water when hooked, rainbows can supply the thrill of a lifetime to a visiting angler. Although no longer being stocked in Lake George by the State, a small population remains.

Landlocked Atlantic Salmon — Atlantic Salmon are internationally known for their impressive fighting ability, which often includes a number of jumps completely out of the water. The Atlantic salmon found in Lake George spend their entire lives in freshwater and are usually called landlocked salmon. Since landlocked salmon are found in different areas of the lake during different seasons, anglers use a wide variety of techniques and tackle at different times of the year. Although natural reproduction does occur to a limited degree, New York State has, for many years, maintained an Atlantic salmon stocking program for Lake George to ensure a desirable population level.

Rainbow Trout (NYSDEC).

Landlocked Atlantic Salmon (NYSDEC).

Lake Trout — Lake trout are a native New York species found in deep cold-water lakes, including the Finger Lakes and Lake George. Like the landlocked salmon, lake trout can be found in different areas of the lake at different times of the year. Similarly, a number of different techniques and tackle are used in their pursuit. Unlike the salmon, however, the stocking of lake trout in Lake George is no longer necessary — the direct result of a number of size-limit increases regulated by New York State.

Lake Trout (NYSDEC).

Fish images originally prepared by Ellen Edmonson and Hugh Chrisp as part of the 1927 to 1940 NY Biological Survey. Permission for use granted by the NYS Department of Environmental Conservation.

Commercial Fishing Guides

Numerous excellent commercial fishing guides are available on Lake George. These guides are licensed by the State of New York. For a list of Lake George fishing guides see page 209.

Kayaking

One of the favored pastimes on Lake George is kayaking. Over the years, kayaking has grown exponentially in popularity and dozens can be seen slicing silently across the lake surface on any given weekend. One of the more popular kayaking locations on the lake is Northwest Bay with its multitude of wildlife. Conveniently, Northwest Bay is also home to a NY State car-top boat launch. The Narrows is another popular kayaking destination, with its maze of islands, shallows, and incredible scenery.

Kayaks are included in the amenities of many of Lake George's resorts and other lodging options. Inquire as to their availability when making your reservations. Kayak rentals, training, and guided kayaking tours are also available.

- **Lake George Kayak Company** (518-644-9366) in Bolton Landing offers kayak rentals, sales, lessons, and guided tours on the lake.
- **Kayak Lake George** (518-302-6005) is located at in Lake George Village at the Shore Meadows Motel and offers kayak rentals.

Kayaking Safety

Lake George is a large lake nestled between steep mountains; consequently, weather and surface conditions can change rapidly. Moreover, during peak weekends, you are sharing the lake with thousands of other boats at any one time, most of which are much larger and faster than you are. To ensure safe and enjoyable kayaking, several safety precautions should be observed.

- Know your limits. If you are new to kayaks and without proper training, stay close to shore. Stay on shore when lake conditions are rough.
- Wear a USCG Approved Type III PFD.
- Check the local weather forecast before heading out.
- Leave a float plan with family or friends for longer outings.
- Although Lake George water is of drinking quality, bring a gallon of water per person to be safe.
- Bring a first aid kit (to include thermal emergency blanket, matches, and energy bars for longer excursions).
- Wear bright colors. Due to their low profile, kayaks can be hard to see from fast moving boats. Don't be afraid to wave a paddle to ensure that you are seen.

• Bring a spare paddle if practical.
• Bring a whistle or air horn to draw attention if assistance is needed.
• Bring a lake map or chart.
• Bring your cell phone in a zip-lock bag or other waterproof container.
• Know how to recover from capsize.

One of the greatest hazards posed to kayak and canoe enthusiasts is hypothermia. As described previously, water temperatures below 60 degrees pose a serious threat. Wear proper clothing designed to retain body heat. Novices should not kayak in cold water.

Sailing

As a life-long sailor, I can attest to the excellent sailing available on Lake George, with long fetches and plenty of deep water. On any given day, the white sails of countless boats can be seen up and down the lake. Sailing on Lake George can nevertheless be challenging. While the prevailing winds on the lake are from north or south, they can often be erratic, with sudden changes in speed and direction common due to the steep mountains rising above both shores of the lake.

Plenty of deep-water dockage is readily available around the lake, at most marinas, restaurants, resorts, and motels. Be sure to ask prior to making your dinner or camping reservations.

Several of the lake's marinas and other facilities offer various services focusing on sailboats. In Middleworth Bay at Diamond Point, **Yankee Boating Center** (518-668-5696) is a full-service marina offering sailboat rentals, parts, and sales.

Sailing lessons are also available at the **"Y-Knot" Sailing School** (518-656-9462) held at the **YMCA Camp Chingachgook** on Pilot Knob, and at the Lake George Yacht Club (members only) at Diamond Point. At the north end of Lake George, the **Northern Lake George Yacht Club** in Hague (nlgyc. com) offers lessons and sailboat racing with adult and junior programs.

The **Canoe Island Lodge** (518-668-5592) offers sailing to their guests on their custom 31-foot sailboats.

Stand Up Paddleboarding (SUP)

If you enjoy being outdoors and on the water, then the ever-increasingly popular sport of stand up paddling is an activity you might want to try. **Stand Up**

Paddling, or **SUP** for short, gets its' roots from the Hawaiian Islands. A stand up board is a long and wide stable board on which you stand, and use a single blade paddle to propel yourself through the water. SUP is a diverse sport; as it lends itself to *stand up paddle surfing, flat water paddling, racing*, and even *white water stand up* for those brave and extreme sport enthusiasts. One of the more inviting aspects of this new sport is that everyone can learn to SUP — whether you are 5 or 85 years of age. Even dogs are taking part and are often seen boarding with their owners.

Stand up paddleboards are available in a variety of sizes and designs. The size of the board is often based on your height and weight. From there, the design of the board is based on the type of water on which you plan to paddle. With all this in mind; it is important to speak to a qualified paddle shop when looking for the right board. It is highly recommended that you always try before you buy.

As with any sport, safety is the first priority. The US Coast Guard has classified SUPs as vessels and users are required to wear or carry a personal floatation device. For those who resist wearing a standard PFD, a waist pack is available that has a self-pull handle that triggers a CO_2 cartridge to inflate the PFD. Paddlers on these low-profile boards can be difficult to see by other boaters, so be sure to wear bright colors and always be aware of other boaters in your vicinity. For the novice, stick to the coves, shoreline, and other more protected areas of the lake, and most importantly, know your limitations.

There are several businesses on the lake that offer SUP rentals including Patty's Water Sports Boutique at Boats by George in Cleverdale, and the Lake George Kayak Company in Bolton Landing.

Special thanks go to Patty Pensel at Patty's Water Sports Boutique. If you would like to learn more about SUP give her a call at 518-656-9353.

A paddleboarder heads out on the lake. Photo by Scott Padeni

Lake George's Southern Basin to Diamond Point

The southern basin of Lake George is home to Lake George Village. The actual population of the Village is just under 4,000. During the summer months, however, this number can swell to over 50,000 as tourists are drawn to the wealth of attractions, accommodations, nightlife and special events that the Village offers. Historically, Lake George's south shore was a major military site during both the French and Indian War (1755–1763) and American Revolution (1775–1783), as is evidenced by the numerous historic sites located there including Fort William Henry and Fort George. This location was later made famous by James Fenimore Cooper's *Last of the Mohicans*. The first permanent settlement occurred at the south end of the lake in 1810 and was named Caldwell after its founder James Caldwell. It held this name until being renamed Lake George Village in 1962.

Lake George Village, view down Canada Street on a summer evening. Photo courtesy Carl Heilman II

The Southern Basin

▌Navigation

Navigating Lake George's southern basin is fairly straightforward. Few shoals and obstructions exist in this portion of the lake, and most that do pose a hazard to boaters are clearly marked. Shallows can be found along the western shore from Tea Island south to Pine Point, and along the lake's south shore west of the Lake George Steamboat Company docks. The boundaries of these shallow areas are marked with white can and/or spar buoys. Two particularly shallow sand-and-gravel deltas extend into the lake in these areas at the mouths of English and West Brooks and are each marked with a white can with orange bands and a diamond (cans "Y" and "Z"). Shoals can also be found at the south end of Tea Island, and just east of Harman Point to the north. Cans and spars also mark these shoals. An isolated shoal can be found on the east shore of the southern basin north of Wiawaka.

Never pass between a hazard buoy and nearby shoreline, or between a hazard can and its associated spars.

● The southwest corner of the lake's south basin is a no wake zone with a speed limit of 5 mph. A line of white and orange regulational spars marks this zone, which runs from the south shore, just east of the Lake George Steamboat Company Pier, roughly along a north-south line with Tea Island. Personal Watercraft (PWCs) are prohibited from operating within this 5 mph zone. Another 5 mph zone exists around Tea Island. Be aware that the speed limit in these zones is strictly enforced.

● The greatest hazard to navigating in Lake George's southern basin arises from the large number of boats operating in this portion of the lake. Lake George Village is a hub of aquatic activity, and during many events such as the weekly fireworks, boats in the southern basin can number in the hundreds. The Village is also homeport to parasailing and large excursion vessels. Be particularly cautious not to impede the passage of these craft, as their speed is often deceiving and their maneuverability is often limited.

▌Anchoring, Docking, Mooring and Marinas

Composition of the lake bottom in the south basin varies but generally consists of sand or mud. Water depths average 40 feet but begin to drop off as you head north. To avoid heavy boat traffic or becoming a speed bump for an excursion vessel, anchoring is best in the southeast corner of the south basin, north of Million Dollar Beach, or along the west shore between English Brook and Tea Island.

Be sure to stay clear of restricted swimming zones, and at least 200 feet offshore from private property.

● Public docking in the Village is located in the southwest corner of the lake just southeast of the Shoreline Cruises excursion boats. Dockage fees are $2.00/hr. with a 10 consecutive hour maximum. Dock space is always at a premium and works on a first-come, first-serve basis, so you may want to arrive early. Pay close attention to your time ashore, since exceeding your time will result in a $25 fine. Rafting, overnight docking (midnight–7:00 am), and use of the docks by commercial vessels is prohibited. These docks are conveniently located near public restrooms, trolley stops, and within easy walking distance to most Village shopping, restaurants, and attractions. Many of the waterfront eateries also offer free dockage for patrons, and an additional hourly fee if you care to explore local attractions following your meal.

Several marinas are also available in the southern basin.

● On the west shore of the Village you will find *Shoreline Marina & Restaurant*, home of U-Drive Boat Rentals (518-668-4644).

97

● ***The Boardwalk Restaurant & Marina*** (518-668-5324) is located a short distance north and offers several amenities including temporary docking, fuel, marine pump-out, and public restrooms for patrons. Dockage is free for restaurant patrons, or for a small hourly fee if you choose to explore ashore. For docking information call 518-668-4828. The Boardwalk marina is a Boat U.S. cooperating marina.

● ***Halls Boat Corporation*** (518-668-5437) is a center for classic & antique boats located on the east shore just east of Million Dollar Beach, with restoration/repair services and full marina service including fuel and seasonal concierge dockage.

● ***Adirondack Marine*** (518-668-2658) is located on the west shore about 2 ½ miles north of the Village providing a ski shop, as well as boat sales and repairs at their service center (518-668-5535).

▌Ashore

Lodging

A detailed listing of available lodging in the Lake George Village area would take an entire volume in itself. Hundreds of options are available ranging from relatively inexpensive motels, efficiencies, rustic cottages to all-inclusive resorts. Listed below are shore-side accommodations, with most offering dockage to their patrons. Be sure to inquire about dockage and launching when making your reservations. The vast majority of these locations are found on the west shore.

● Beginning at the south end of the lake is the ***Fort William Henry Hotel and Conference Center*** (518-668-3081) just across the street from the public docks. This large hotel offers numerous amenities and is located adjacent to the fort (whose name it bears), in the heart of Lake George Village.

● In the Village along the west shore is the ***Marine Village Resort*** (518-668-5478), offering 98 rooms including 5 lake front suites, breakfast restaurant, kayak, canoes, paddleboats and dockage for both seasonal boat owners and guests. Expansive beach, patio and pool areas are available and are home for daily resort sponsored activities and cook outs.

- Just to the north is the *Lake Crest Inn* (518-668-3374). Amenities of the Lake Crest Inn include motel rooms and suites, sandy beach, breakfast and lunch, rowboats and kayaks. Seasonal dockage available.

- Continuing north, the *Park Lane Motel* (518-668-2615) offers rooms with kitchenettes, pool, beach, kayaks, paddlebords, paddle boats, gas grills, and limited boat dockage.

- One of the more elegant lodging options at the south end of the lake is the *Georgian Lakeside Resort* (518-668-5870). The Georgian offers conference facilities, motel rooms, suites, large pool, sandy beach, paddleboats and kayaks. They also have a restaurant and bar on site. No dockage available.

- *Surfside on the Lake* (518-668-2442) has hotel rooms and suites, on-site restaurant, large beach, pool, kayaks, and paddleboats. No dockage.

- *O'Sullivans-on-the-Lake Motel* (518-668-5424) has both motel rooms and apartments. They also have a sandy beach, kayaks, rowboats, and dockage available.

- To the north is the *Sundowner Motel* (518-668-5175) providing motel rooms, pool, beach, and kayaks for guests. No dockage available.

- *Shore Meadows Motel* (518-668-3366) is just to the north and has motel rooms and cottages, sandy beach and dockage for guests. Shore Meadows is also home to Kayak Lake George for kayak rentals.

- Nearby *Scotty's Lakeside Resort* (518-668-2467) has over 100 motel rooms, lounge, snack bar, beach, and numerous other amenities. They also have dockage and a boat launch for guests.

Three quarters of a mile north along the bay near Tea Island, several additional lodging options are available:

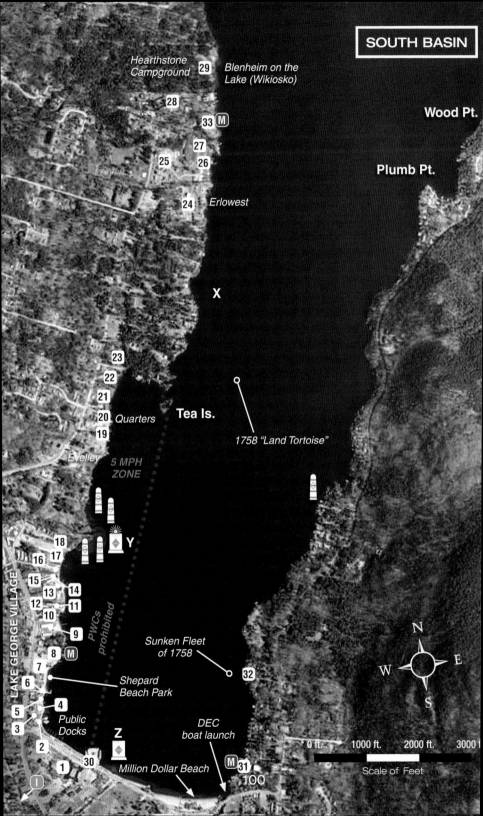

SOUTH BASIN

Hearthstone Campground 29
Blenheim on the Lake (Wikiosko)
Wood Pt.
28
33 Ⓜ
Plumb Pt.
27
25 26
24 Erlowest
X
23
22
21
20 Quarters
19 Tea Is.
Evelley
1758 "Land Tortoise"
5 MPH ZONE
Y
18
16 17
15
13 14
12 11
10
9
Sunken Fleet of 1758
8 Ⓜ
7
6 Shepard Beach Park
5
3 Public Docks
Z
4
2 DEC boat launch
1 30 Ⓜ 31
Million Dollar Beach 100

32

PWCs prohibited

LAKE GEORGE VILLAGE

N
W E
S

0 ft. 1000 ft. 2000 ft. 3000
Scale of Feet

South Basin map key

1 Fort William Henry Hotel and Conference Center

2 Lake George Parasailing Adventures

3 Shoreline Restaurant, Shoreline Cruises & King Neptune's Pub

4 Christie's on the Lake

5 Parasail Joe's

6 Shepard's Cove

7 Lake George Historical Association and Museum

8 Boardwalk Restaurant and Marina

9 Marine Village Resort

10 Lake Crest Inn

11 Park Lane Motel

12 Lake Motel

13 Georgian Lakeside Resort

14 Surfside on the Lake

15 O'Sullivans-on-the-Lake Motel

16 Sundowner Motel

17 Shore Meadows Motel

18 Scotty's Lakeside Resort

19 Tahoe Resort

20 Quarters on Lake George

21 Tea Island Resort

22 Boulders Resort

23 Alpine Village

24 Inn at Erlowest

25 Lodges at Cresthaven

26 Boathouse Restaurant

27 Bayfront Cottages

28 Clinton Inn

29 Hearthstone Public Campground

30 Lake George Steamboat Company

31 Halls Boat Corporation

32 Wiawaka Holiday House

33 Adirondack Marine

🅜 Marina

🅘 Inspection station

Twilight on Lake George. Photo courtesy Shoreline Cruises

- The expansive *Tahoe Resort* (518-668-5711) offers motel rooms, large sandy beach, pool, and numerous other amenities.

- Just north of the Tahoe is *Quarters on Lake George* (518-668-4901). The Quarters is a four-season resort and one of the more luxurious on the lake. The centerpiece of the resort is the 19th century mansion once owned by American photographer Alfred Stieglitz and his wife, the famed American artist Georgia O'Keefe. The resort offers a wide range of amenities including luxury suites, fitness center, indoor pool, beach and dockage for their guests.

- The *Tea Island Resort* (518-668-2776) is nestled on the cove behind tea island. In addition to motel rooms and cottages, they offer complementary kayaks, canoes, paddle boards, row boats, paddleboats, playground, volleyball and badminton. They also have dockage available for both seasonal boat owners and guests.

- The nearby *Boulders Resort* (518-668-5444) also offers cottages, townhouses, and efficiency motel rooms. Amenities include a sandy beach, boat dockage, picnic areas with grills, pools, hot tub, playgrounds, gamerooms, rowboats, canoes, kayaks and paddleboats.

- At the north end of the cove you will find the rustic *Alpine Village* (518-668-2193). The Alpine Village offers classic Adirondack log cabins, a beach, and dockage. They also have an onsite breakfast restaurant, which is boat accessible and open to the public.

- A half-mile north is the luxurious *Inn at Erlowest* (518-668-5928) and *Sun Castle Resort* (518-668-2085). The Inn at Erlowest offers elegant lodging and inspired cuisine, along with large event capability for weddings and corporate events. Prominent Brooklyn Attorney Edward Morse Shepard built Erlowest in 1898. On the grounds of Erlowest is the Sun Castle Resort, offering beautiful townhouses and villas with a wide array of luxury amenities and on-site activities including complimentary kayaks and a heated pool. Both have an expansive beach, dockage, and a boat launch for guests.

- Located just north is *The Lodges at Cresthaven* (518-668-3332). This beautiful Gold Crown resort is located one mile north of Lake George Village. The Lodges boasts luxurious family Adirondack lodges with fractional ownership or rentals available. The lodges boasts many amenities including a private beach, indoor/outdoor pools, fitness room, playground, video game room, volleyball, badminton, bocce, horseshoe pits, barbeque grills, and seasonal entertainment and activities. The Boathouse restaurant is located on the same property.

- Continuing north, *Bayfront Cottages* (518-668-9579) provides 10 rustic cottages, waterside pavilion, expansive beach, and dockage for guests.

- Just south of the Hearthstone Campground, is the *Clinton Inn* (518-668-2412) offering cottages and motel rooms, onsite breakfast and lunch restaurant, tennis courts, putting green, and sandy beach. No dockage available.

- For campers, *Hearthstone Public Campground* (518-668-5193) is located 2 ½ miles north of the Village on the lake's west shore. For a fee of $22 per night, Hearthstone offers 251 tent and trailer sites, hot showers, flush toilets, sand beach with life guard and a designated swimming area. There are no boat launch facilities, docks, or moorings at Hearthstone. However, those camping along the shoreline often anchor their boats in front of their campsites, with a stern line running to shore for added security. Use caution if you choose to use such a technique, as Hearthstone is exposed to the open lake providing no shelter from wind and waves.

- On the opposite side of the lake from the village, several lodging options are available. *Halls Boat Corporation* (518-668-5437) offers several weekly-rental Adirondack-style lake houses, each available with use of a boat slip.

- Two miles up the lake on the east shore is the *Wiawaka Holiday House* (1-877-468-8128). Wiawaka was established in 1903 during the women's rights movement to provide a retreat for the overworked women of the Troy, NY collar industry. This nonprofit is the oldest remaining retreat on the lake today, and offers affordable vacations and enrichment programs to women 18 or older.

Dining

Dining options also abound in the Village and range from fast food to gourmet dining. Most are within walking distance of the Village public docks. Several of these eateries are on the water's edge and have docks for their patrons.

Situated on the southwest corner of the lake, the *Shoreline Restaurant* (518-668-4644) offers a relaxing atmosphere, a full-service bar, and large covered patio overlooking the lake. Their menu includes both fine and casual dining. Next door you will find the Shoreline's sister establishment, *King Neptune's Pub* (518-668-2017), offering pub fare and live music in their main room and on their rooftop deck. For those seeking nightlife, King Neptune's is known as one of the lake's hot spots with music and dancing continuing well into the wee hours. Both establishments are located only a few hundred feet from the public docks.

Adjacent to the north is *Christie's on the Lake* (518-668-2515). Christie's offers both casual and fine dining, live entertainment, and multi-level outdoor patios overlooking the lake, a short walk from the public docks.

Shepard's Cove (518-668-4988) is located at the south end of Shepard's Park Beach, with their patron docks situated just south of the pedestrian pier. Shepard's cove offers an extensive menu, an upper and lower deck overlooking the lake, and late night entertainment on weekends.

Just north of Shepard Park Beach is the *Boardwalk Restaurant and Marina* (518-668-5324). The Boardwalk also offers both casual and fine dining, and has an enclosed first floor dining room, covered upper patio with live entertainment, and open boathouse deck. The Boardwalk's marina (518-668-4828) has ample dockage for patrons, as well as fuel and pump-out facilities.

Tucked in the cove just west of Tea Island, the *Alpine Village Resort's* (518-668-2193) breakfast restaurant is one of the best-kept secrets in the village. Their restaurant has dockage available for patrons.

Two miles up the west shore of the lake is the *Inn at Erlowest* (518-668-5928) offering gourmet dining in one of the most beautiful mansions on Millionaires Row. Brooklyn lawyer and socialite Edward Morse Shepard built the large Queen Anne Style stone castle in 1898. Sixteen docks are available for patrons. Call in advance to reserve space.

A short distance north, the *The Boathouse Restaurant, at the Lodges at Cresthaven* (800-853-1632), also offers fine dining in an upscale atmosphere. Enjoy splendid water's edge dining on the newly restored outside terrace. Sip frosty beverages at the outside bar overlooking Lake George. Specialties include juicy Angus steaks and burgers, fresh seafood, pasta and creative nightly specials. Also available for special events. This elegant restaurant was originally built in 1876 as part of the Abenin estate, owned by *New York Times* Publisher Adolph Ochs. The mansion burned in the 1950s, though the boathouse survived. Dockage is available for guests.

Most of these restaurants maintain limited hours during May and June, and after Labor Day. It would be wise to call in advance.

Entertainment and Attractions

Attractions and entertainment options in Lake George Village are seemingly endless with something for everyone on your crew. Many of these activities are located within walking distance of the Village's public docks, or along the Lake George Trolley route. For the history lover a visit to *Fort William Henry* is only a short walk from the public docks. This reproduction fort is based on the original fort built in 1755 during the French and Indian War (1755–1763) and later made famous by James Fenimore Cooper's *Last of the Mohicans.*

Less than a half-mile east from the public docks along Beach Road you will find *Lake George Battlefield Park*. This park was the location of the Battle of Lake George fought in 1755. Paved trails and interpretive signage guide you through the park's historic points including the ruins of Fort George, built in 1759.

The **Lake George Historical Association and Museum** is located in the Old Warren County Court House building on Canada Street near Shepard Park, offering numerous displays focusing on Lake George history.

Other nearby attractions include several miniature golf courses, excursion boat tours, a wax museum, Dr. Morbid's Haunted House, numerous arcades, ice cream shops, and even horse drawn carriage rides. Public beaches in the Village include Million Dollar beach and Shepard Park Beach. Boats are not allowed to approach the shore at either of these beaches; however both are within walking distance of the public docks. Ushers Park Beach is on the east shore. This small park and shallow beach make it ideal for small children. For the more adventurous, parasailing is another popular attraction offered in the Village. Flights can be arranged at kiosks located along the boardwalk. Talk to Mike at **Lake George Parasailing Adventures** (518-668-9234), located just north of the public boat docks. **Parasail Joe's** (518-668-4013) can be found a short distance north at their National Water Sports kiosk.

Boat rentals are also available in the Village at *Shoreline Marina (U-Drive Boats), National Water Sports.* Pontoon boats and runabouts can be rented from *Lake George Boat Rentals.* See page 208 for a completed listing of boat rental agents on Lake George.

A must-see for boaters on Lake George are the **fireworks** displays provided weekly in the Village. The fireworks are launched from a barge stationed several hundred feet offshore, providing a spectacular front-row seat for boaters. Use care during these events, however, since boats often number in the hundreds and their mass exodus at the show's conclusion can be somewhat challenging in the dark. Always check the operation of your navigation lights before setting off. Fireworks displays are provided in the village every Thursday night from July to August, and on July 4th.

Watch for other annual events hosted in the Village:

May	Memorial Day Weekend
May–June	E.S.T.R.A. Tow Truck Show
May–June	Lake George Vintage Raceboat Regatta
June	Prospect Mountain POW/MIA Memorial Service
June	Americade Motorcycle Touring Rally
June	Lake George Area Restaurant Week
June–Sept	Friday Night Concerts in Shepard Park
June	Father's Day Brunch and Dinner Cruises
June	Firemen's Association Convention
June	Summerfest & Arts and Crafts Show
June	Adirondack Distance Run
July–Aug	Magical Musical Mondays in Shepard Park
July	4th of July Celebration
July–Sept	Fireworks Thursday nights at 9:30 pm
July	The Big Apple Circus
July	Lake George Music Festival

July	Lake George Hot Rod Happening
Aug	Lake George Arts & Crafts Festival
Aug	Lake George Rendezvous Antique & Classic Boat Show
Aug–Sept	Labor Day Weekend Celebrations
Sept	Adirondack Nationals Car Show
Sept	Lake George Village Jazz Festival
Sept	Adirondack Balloon Festival
Sept	Lake George Triathlon Festival
Oct	Oktoberfest and Craft Show

Shopping

Abundant shopping is also available in the Village. As with any resort area, numerous T-shirt, gift, and souvenir shops are plentiful along Canada Street and Beach Road within only a few blocks. Other shops include specialty boutiques, jewelry stores, museum shops, and galleries selling items made by local artisans. Numerous outlet stores can be found several miles south on Route 9.

For boaters seeking ground transportation, the Lake George Trolley system is available during the summer months from the last weekend in June until Labor Day with two routes running every half hour from the public docks. The trolley's north service runs to Bolton Landing and points in between including Hearthstone Park; its south service runs as far as Glens Falls with stops including the outlet stores and Six Flags Amusement Park. Fares are $1.00 for adults, and free for children under 5. Transfers between trolleys are 50 cents.

Antique and Classic Boat Show. Photo by Peggy Huckel

The Southeast Bays: Dunham's, Warner, Harris, Sandy, and Kattskill Bays

Several prominent bays including Dunham's Bay, Harris Bay, Warner Bay, Sandy Bay, and Kattskill Bay dominate the southeast portion of Lake George. These Bays are oriented generally north to south and are separated by two points of land — Assembly Point and Cleverdale.

▌Navigation

Dunham's Bay, situated on the south side of Assembly Point, is the southernmost of these bays. Navigation within Dunham's Bay is not difficult, though there are several hazards to be avoided. To the southwest, a shoal found just off Woods Point is marked by a spar buoy. At the western flank of Dunham's Bay several partially exposed shoals are located along the east shore of Diamond Island. Often referred to as Dick's Islands, these shoals are extremely shallow and have claimed many an unwary boater. The southernmost shoal is marked by spars and lighted can "W2." The northern most shoal is marked by spars and lighted can buoy "W2A." Remember to NOT pass between can buoys and their associated spars. Approximately ¼ mile southeast of Diamond Island, another shoal is marked by lighted can buoy "W."

Another set of buoys about a quarter mile east of Diamond Island is not a shoal, but rather marks the LG Underwater Heritage Preserve site of the shipwreck "Forward." The buoys consist of a lighted white can bouy, and a white and blue spherical mooring buoy several feet away.

Two small shoals can be found along the north shore of Dunham's Bay where Assembly point meets the mainland. Unlit obstruction spars mark these shoals. Also be aware that a five-mile per hour zone exists in the lower southeast portion of Dunham's Bay, which is strictly enforced. Access to Dunham's Bay Brook and Dunham's Bay Marina is via a marked channel leading under the Route 9L bridge. This bridge has a maximum clearance of 59 inches above lake surface. Motorized vehicles are prohibited from operating on Dunham's Bay Brook beyond a point approximately 2,000 feet from the Route 9L bridge.

The shortest route north to Harris and Warner Bays will take you through the narrow channel between Long Island and Assembly point. Navigate this channel cautiously as this is one of the busier bottlenecks on the lake and a favorite route of several of the large excursion vessels. When approaching the channel from the south, you will note several obstruction buoys off your port side marking shoals at the southern tip of Speaker Heck Island. These buoys include several spars, with the southernmost consisting of lighted can buoy "U2." At this point the channel drops to a 5 mph zone. Continuing north, you will pass between the southern tip of Long Island to your port and Assembly point to starboard. Be sure to stay within the channel, as it is flanked on both sides by shoals that are marked by obstruction buoys including lighted can buoy "U1"to starboard.

DO NOT attempt to pass between the gap between Speaker Heck and Long Islands. Depths in this gap only range from 1 to 2 feet.

For deeper drafted vessels, stay clear of Hogback Reef just off the northwest end of Long Island. This elongated shoal rises to approximately 6 feet below the surface and is marked by an unlit white obstruction can. This is a great location for snorkeling and diving as the shoal serves as home to a wide range of fish.

Harris Bay is bounded to the west by Assembly Point, to the east by Cleverdale and to the northwest by Long Island. The southern half-mile of Harris Bay is limited to 5 mph. Moreover, extreme care should be taken to follow

Southeast Bays map key

1	Antigua Resort	**9**	Cleverdale Post Office
2	Dunham's Bay Marina 🅸	**10**	Cleverdale Country Store
3	Dunham's Bay Boat Company	**11**	Castaway Marina
4	Dunham's Bay Lake George Resort (View Bar and Restaurant & The Bear Room Lounge)	**12**	Fischer's Marina
		13	Pilot Knob Marina
5	Harris Bay Yacht Club	**14**	Camp Chingachgook
6	Lake George Boat Company	**15**	Speaker Heck Day-Use Island
7	Sans Souci Restaurant	**16**	Long Island Campground
8	Boats By George and Patty's Water Sports Boutique	**17**	Long Island Ranger Station
		18	Diamond Island Day-Use Site

🅸 Inspection station   Ⓜ Marina

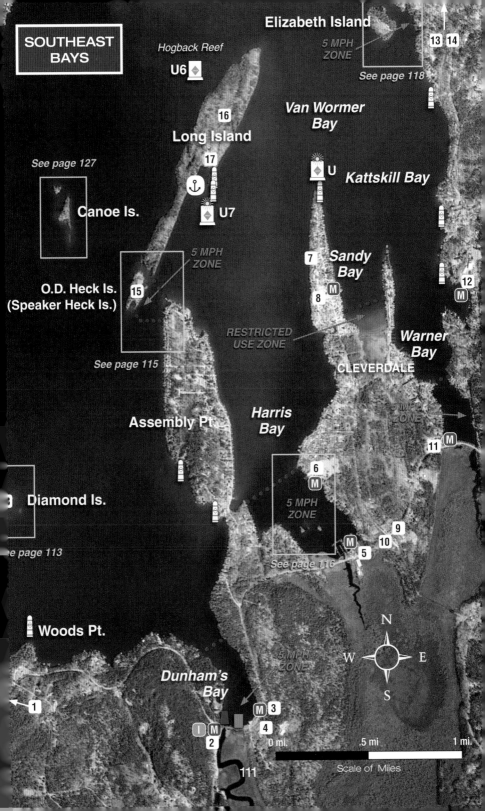

SOUTHEAST
BAYS

Elizabeth Island

Hogback Reef

U6

5 MPH
ZONE

See page 118

13 14

16

Van Wormer
Bay

Long Island

17

U

Kattskill Bay

See page 127

Canoe Is.

U7

7

Sandy
Bay

O.D. Heck Is.
(Speaker Heck Is.)

5 MPH
ZONE

15

8

M

12

M

RESTRICTED
USE ZONE

Warner
Bay

See page 115

CLEVERDALE

Assembly Pt

Harris
Bay

5 MPH
ZONE

11

M

Diamond Is.

6

M

5 MPH
ZONE

9

10

ee page 113

See page 116

5

M

Woods Pt.

N

1

Dunham's
Bay

5 MPH
ZONE

W   E

M   3

S

I   M

4

2

0 mi.   .5 mi.   1 mi.

111

Scale of Miles

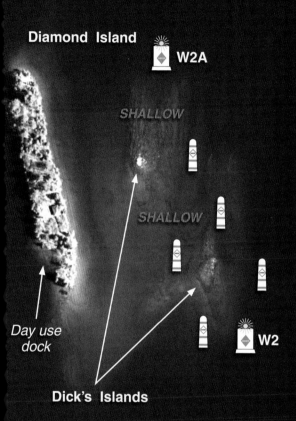

DIAMOND
ISLAND

N
W · E
S

Diamond Island

 W2A

SHALLOW

SHALLOW

The "Forward"
wreck, underwater
classroom

Day use
dock

W2

Dick's Islands

SHOALS

W

0 ft.   250 ft.   500 ft.

Scale of Feet

Bow of the sunken 1906 watercraft *Forward*. Photo courtesy Dr. Russell Bellico/Bateau Below

Diamond Island

Diamond Island is a state owned picnic island. Its name comes from the six-sided quartz crystals found on the island. In the 19th century, these rocks were sold in New York City as "Lake George Diamonds." However the true richness of Diamond Island is its history. During the the French and Indian War and American Revolution the island was used as a military outpost because of its strategic location in the center of the lake, 3 miles from the lake's south end. During the Revolution, General John Burgoyne's British army used the island as a supply depot. In September 1777, American forces led by Col. John Brown attacked the island with 20 boats that he had captured at the north end of the lake. During what is known as the "Battle of Diamond Island," Brown's force of 420 men attacked on Sept. 24th but was soon repulsed by the firepower of 12-pounder cannon manned by two companies of the British 47th regiment. With 10 men dead, numerous wounded, and one of his vessels sunk, Brown and his battered flotilla were forced to retreat into Dunham's Bay where he beached his boats and burned them to prevent their capture by the British. Brown and his men escaped to rejoin the American army. Several weeks later on October 17, General Burgoyne and his entire army would surrender at the Battle of Saratoga, considered the turning point of the American Revolution, and one of the 15 most decisive battles in world history.

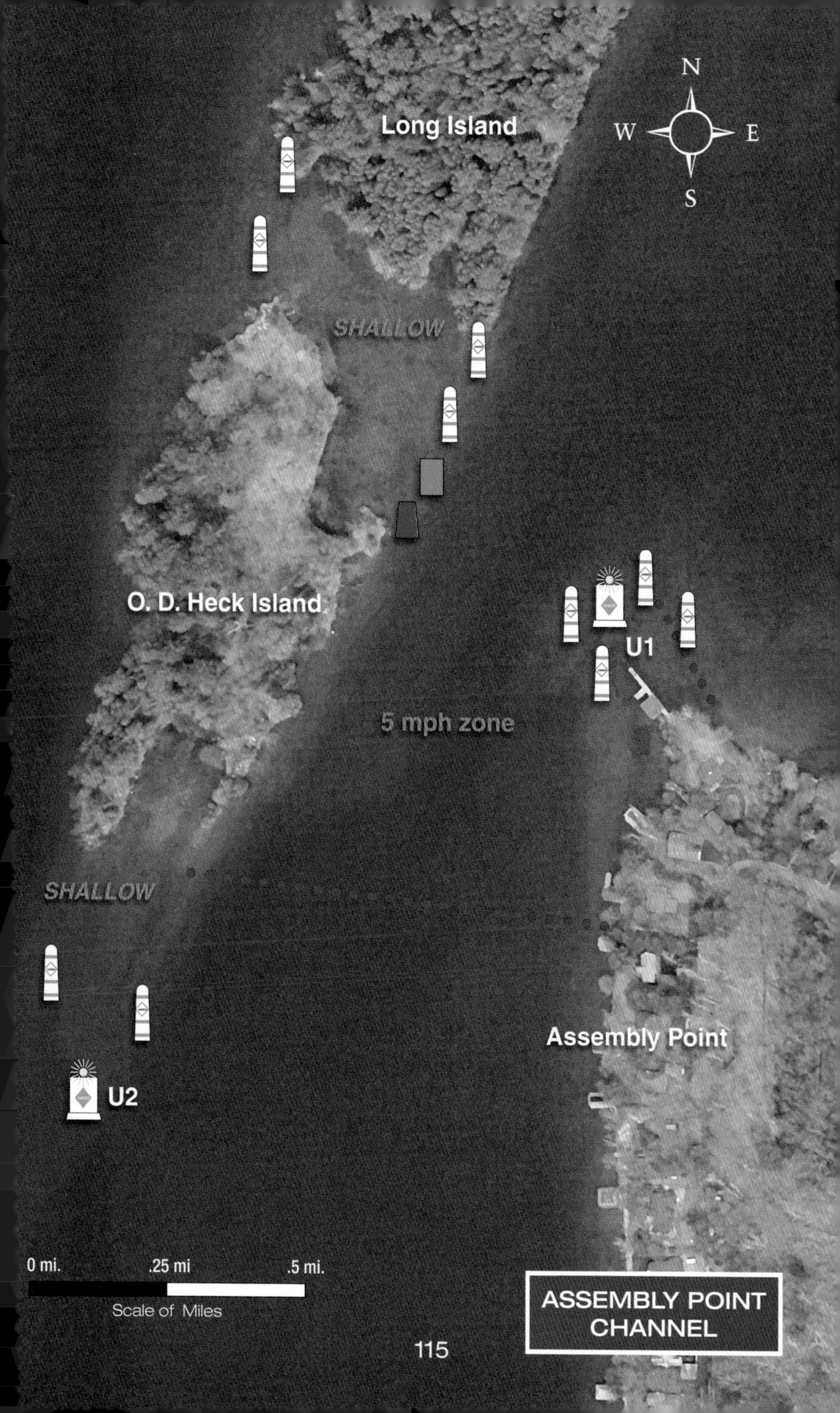

Long Island

N
W   E
S

SHALLOW

O. D. Heck Island

U1

5 mph zone

SHALLOW

U2

Assembly Point

0 mi.   .25 mi   .5 mi.

Scale of Miles

**ASSEMBLY POINT
CHANNEL**

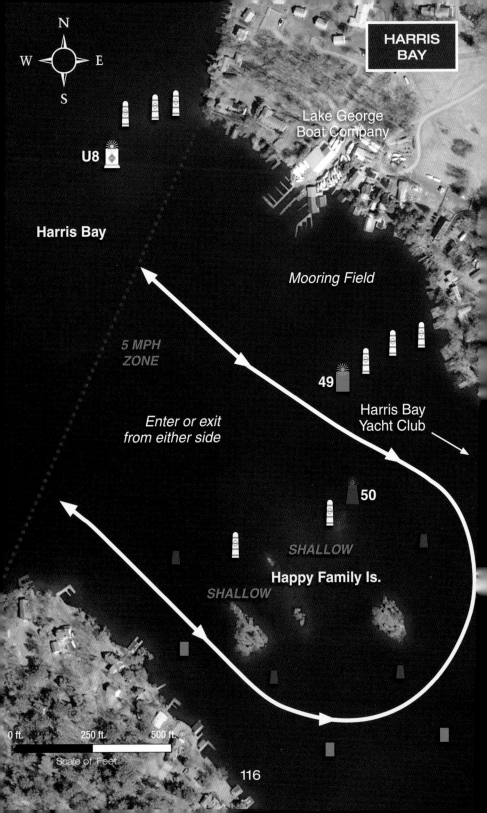

HARRIS BAY

N
W E
S

Lake George
Boat Company

U8

Harris Bay

Mooring Field

5 MPH
ZONE

Enter or exit
from either side

49

Harris Bay
Yacht Club

50

SHALLOW

Happy Family Is.

SHALLOW

0 ft.   250 ft.   500 ft.

Scale of Feet

the channels surrounding the rocky outcroppings known as the Happy Family Islands. Stay between the green and red buoys marking these channels, and be sure to avoid the obstruction buoys that also mark the nearby shoals. Be particularly cautious on the west side of these islands and shoals since one or two spars marked on charts are missing.

Another large submerged shoal is located at the northeast corner of the 5 mph zone several hundred feet northwest of the Lake George Boat Company marina. This shoal extends over 350 feet off the east shore and is marked by obstruction spars, with lighted can "U8" marking its west extremity. As always, be sure not to pass between these markers and the shoreline.

To the northeast of Harris Bay on the opposite side of Cleverdale, lies Kattskill Bay leading south into Sandy and Warner Bays. A 5 mph zone marks the southern ends of both. The few hazards to navigation in these bays consist of several isolated shoals north along the east shore of Warner Bay and Kattskill Bays. A shoal, marked by obstruction spars and lighted can "U," is located off Ripley Point at the north end of Cleverdale.

At the northern end of Kattskill Bay you will come to Elizabeth Island and three small bays at the base of Pilot Knob Mountain. The narrow passage between privately owned Elizabeth Island and the mainland is a designated 5 mph zone. Stay clear of shoals between the island and Travis Point by using the channel marked by lighted green and red buoys. North of Elizabeth Island are Echo, Isom, and Barber Bays. Use care if visiting these small picturesque bays since islets and/or submerged obstructions mark their entrances.

∎ Anchoring, Docking, Mooring and Marinas

There are numerous locations in this vicinity of the lake suitable for anchoring depending on wind direction and lake conditions. When choosing an anchorage, keep in mind that these bays are exposed to the weather in a north to northwest wind. Also remember not to anchor within 200 feet of private property. Some of the more popular anchorages include the southeastern portion of Harris Bay, Warner Bay, and on the east side of Diamond Island. Another favorite anchorage is in the small bay on the east side of Long Island near the Ranger Station docks. When entering this spot be sure to stay south of lighted can "U7." This can buoy marks the south end of the shoals and islets that form the east side of the bay.

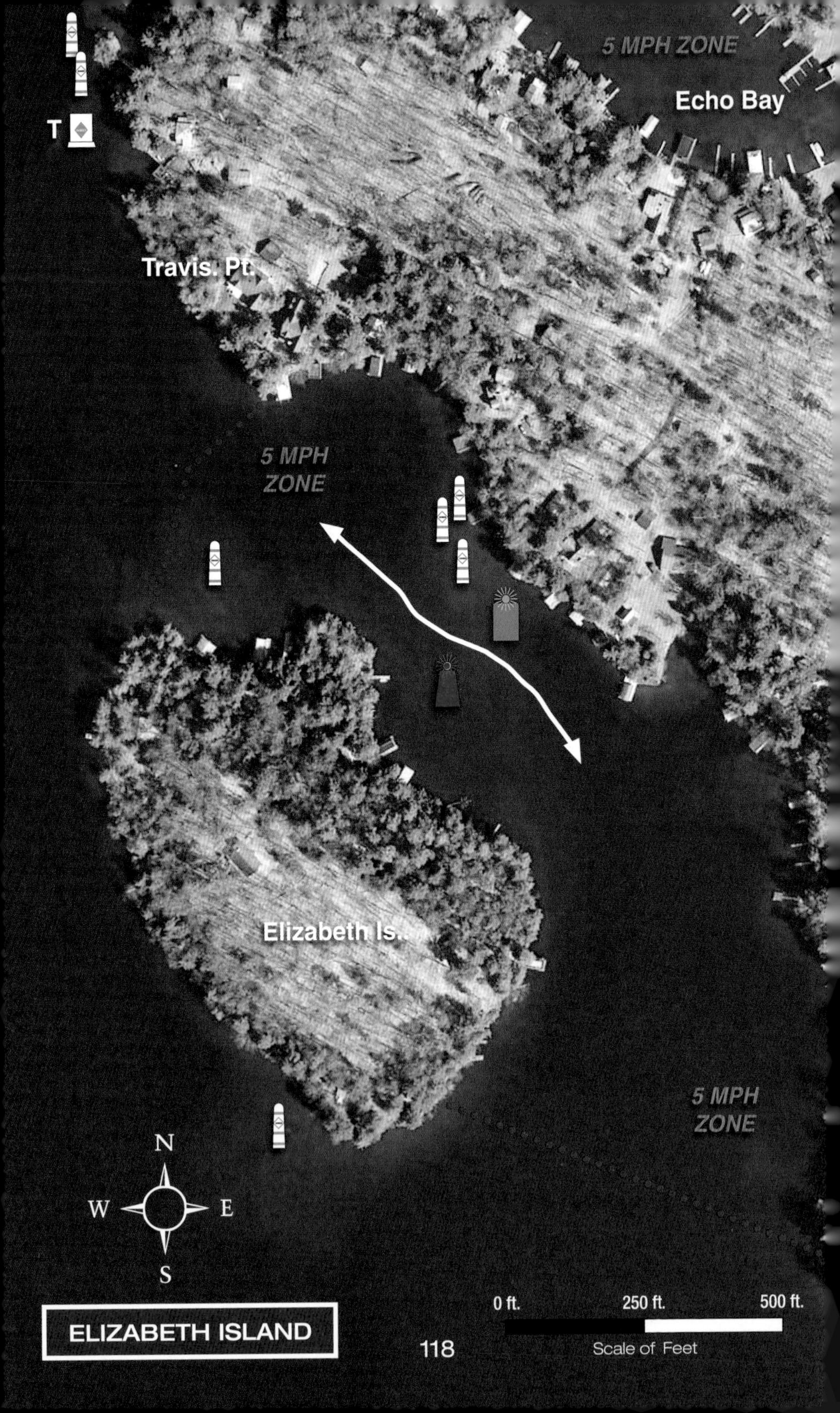

5 MPH ZONE

Echo Bay

T

Travis. Pt.

5 MPH ZONE

5 MPH ZONE

Elizabeth Is.

N
W   E
S

ELIZABETH ISLAND

118

0 ft.   250 ft.   500 ft.

Scale of Feet

● Transient dockage is offered by several of the marinas located in this area, which are listed below. Dockage is also available at several of the nearby state-owned islands including Diamond, Speaker Heck, and Long Islands. Speaker Heck Island (named for O.D. Heck, Speaker of the NY State Legislature between 1937–1951) is located at the south end of Long Island and designated as one of 8 day-use picnic islands on the lake. The island has a picnic shelter with a capacity of 15 people. The picnic shelter can be reserved if you hold an annual day-use pass. The island also has a protected swim area for children at its north end. Dockage is also available at nearby Diamond Island, the southernmost of the day-use picnic islands, and situated only 3 miles north of the Village. Both of these day-use islands come complete with docks, charcoal grills, fireplaces and tables. Dogs are not permitted on any of the state-owned islands, docks, or on boats berthed at island docks. Permits for Diamond and Speaker Heck Islands are available at the ranger station on Long Island. No day-use permits are issued after 8:00 pm, and all visitors must leave the islands by 9:00 pm.

● A public dock is available at the Long Island Ranger station with a time limit of 15 minutes. Dockage is also available with each of the 90 campsites on Long Island. Reservations for these campsites can be made by calling 1-800-456-CAMP (1-800-456-2267) or online at: www.newyorkstateparks.reserveamerica.com.

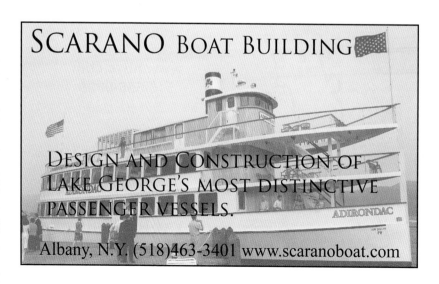

● Public moorings are available in Sandy Bay. The shallow waters and sandy bottom make it a favorite spot among the boating public. If staying in Sandy Bay, use of these moorings is required; they are available on a first-come, first-served basis. **Anchoring, rafting to another vessel, or drifting in the Sandy Bay zone is prohibited.** In addition, vessels cannot be beached except by the owners of adjacent private property. The moorings are closed between sunset and sunrise.

● Several marinas are available in this region of the lake. In Dunham's Bay, ***Dunham's Bay Boat Company*** (518-656-9244) offers gasoline, pump out, restrooms, repairs, a marine store, boat rentals, and boat registrations.

● On the east side of NY State Route 9L you will find ***Dunham's Bay Marina*** (518-744-2627). This marina is situated on Dunham's Bay Brook and provides transient dockage, 24-hour launching facilities, restrooms and boating registrations. Be aware that to access the lake from this marina you must pass under the Route 9L bridge that has an average vertical clearance of 59 inches from the waterline. **This is an official inspection station.**

- At the south end of Harris Bay, the *Harris Bay Yacht Club* (518-656-9028), a full-service marina, has a wide range of services including gasoline, pump out, repairs, launching and haul-out, a marine store, and winter storage. They also provide restrooms, showers, laundry and gas grills for yacht club members and renters.

- *The Lake George Boat Company* (518-656-9203) is also located in the southern basin of Harris Bay and offers quick launch facilities, gasoline, season dockage, moorings, repairs pump out, a ships store, emergency towing, picnic area and showers.

- *Boats By George on the Lake and Patty's Water Sports Boutique* (518-656-9353) is located in Cleverdale on the west shore of Sandy Bay, and provides launch facilities, gasoline, pump out, repairs, a marine store, restrooms, and Lake George boat registrations.

- In Warner Bay, *Castaway Marina* (518-656-3636) is located in the bay's southwest corner, and provides launch facilities, non-ethanol gasoline, pump out, repairs, and marine store, ice, a restroom for customers, and Lake George boat registrations.

- *Fischer's Marina* (518-656-9981) is also located in Kattskill Bay along its east shore. They provide seasonal and aunching facilities including "quick launch," gasoline, pump out, repairs, restrooms, beer and soda, snacks, ice, worms, and firewood. Fischer's also offers boat rentals, emergency towing, and Lake George boat registrations.

● Three miles north, *Pilot Knob Marina* (518-656-9211) can provide gasoline, repairs, restrooms, Lake George boat registrations and a ship's store.

▌ Ashore

Lodging and Camping

Unlike Lake George Village where options for lodging are seemingly limitless, lodging in this region of the lake consists predominantly of camping and cottage rentals.

● Two excellent exceptions include the *Antigua Resort* (518-668-2556) and *Dunham's Bay Lake George Resort* (518-656-9242). The Antigua Resort is located on Plum Point, just southwest of Dunhams Bay. The Antigua offers motel rooms, suites, and a two-bedroom boathouse. They also offer a private sandy beach, rowboats and canoes, an incredible view, and a reputation for being family-oriented. Dockage is available for guests. Dunham's Bay Lake George Resort is located at the south end of Dunham's Bay and offers cabins, hotel rooms, suites, a full service restaurant, and a free shuttle to area attractions. No dockage available.

Listings for the numerous cottage and house rentals available in this area can be found on the local Chamber of Commerce website (www.lakegeorgechamber.com) and from www.lakegeorge.com. For the more adventurous, camping is also available in this section of the Lake.

● Located just 4 ½ miles north of the Village, *Long Island* has over 80 campsites, each with its own dock. Sites located on the east shore of the 100-acre Island typically offer more protection from the weather, while sites on the island's west side offer some of the more spectacular views. Lake conditions on the west side of the island can often get rough, however, so be sure to bring plenty of fenders. For more details, refer to our camping section on pages 43–50.

● YMCA's *Camp Chingachgook* (518-656-9462) is a traditional summer camp offering a wide variety of activities for youngsters including hiking, camping, sailing, fishing, swimming, biking, and more. Their camp is located on the west shore just north of Pilot Knob.

Dining

While there are no dock-and-dine eateries in this part of the lake, there are several eateries available on shore.

- One of these is **Sans Souci** (518-656-9285) in Cleverdale located between Sandy and Harris Bay. Their menu ranges from light pub fare to full dinners.

- The **Cleverdale Country Store** (518-656-9057), located at the intersection of Ridge Road (9L) and Clerverdale Road, is a Lake George treasure featuring an excellent deli, fresh produce, groceries, camping supplies, and countless other goods.

- At the south end of Dunham's Bay the **View Bar and Restaurant,** and **The Bear's Den Lounge** (518-656-9242) are located in the Dunham's Bay Lake George Resort. Both offer light fare, pizzas, full entrees, and more. They also offer boxed lunches or take out for boaters.

Fort William Henry Hotel from the water. Photo by Peggy Huckel.

Diamond Point and Vicinity

Diamond Point is actually part of Lake George, though by most it is considered a separate community, complete with its own zip code and post office. Diamond Point is often favored among vacationing boaters. Its location on the west side of the lake, roughly midway between Lake George Village and Bolton Landing, allows easy access to the attractions of both, while providing a more quiet setting with spectacular views of the lake and surrounding mountains. This area is also home to several of the historic mansions that are part of Millionaires Row along the west shore of the lake.

Diamond Point map key

1	Cramers Point Motel & Cottages	15	Stepping Stones Resort
2	O'Connors Resort Cottages	16	Canoe Island Lodge
3	Still Bay Resort	17	Juliana Resort
4	Depe Dene Resort	18	Thunderbird Resort & Marina
5	Diamond Cove Cottages	19	Yankee Marina
6	Golden Sands Resort	20	Flamingo Resort
7	Mt. Knoll Beach Cottages	21	Capri Village
8	Lake George Suites	22	Treasure Cove
9	Gilchrist Marina and Motel	23	Beckley's Boats
10	Blue Lagoon	24	Lake George Club
11	Pot Beli Deli	25	O.D. Heck Day-Use Island
12	Olympian Village Motel	26	Long Island Campground
13	Diamond Point Grill	27	Long Island Ranger Station
14	Diamond Point Community Beach	28	Diamond Island Day-Use Site

M Marina

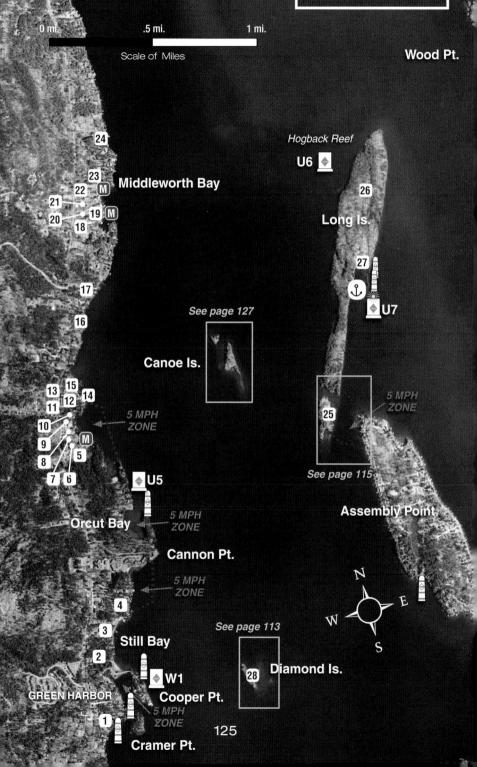

Wood Pt.

0 mi.　　　.5 mi.　　　1 mi.

Scale of Miles

Hogback Reef

U6

24

23

22　M　Middleworth Bay

21

20　19　M

18

26

Long Is.

27

U7

17

16

See page 127

Canoe Is.

13　15

12　14

11

10

9

5

8

5 MPH ZONE

M

5

7　6

25

See page 115

5 MPH ZONE

U5

5 MPH ZONE

Orcut Bay

Assembly Point

Cannon Pt.

5 MPH ZONE

4

3

Still Bay

2

W1

GREEN HARBOR

Cooper Pt.

5 MPH ZONE

1

Cramer Pt.

See page 113

28　Diamond Is.

N
W　E
S

▌Navigation

Few hazards to navigation exist in this region of the lake and most of those that are present are clearly visible or marked by obstruction buoys. Obstructions can be found just north of the Hearthstone Campground beach. There are also shoals along the northeast shoreline of Coopers Point, marked by obstruction spars and an unlit can buoy "W1."

Half a mile north, there is an isolated shoal just off the south shore of Cannon Point. Shoals can also be found at the north tip of Cannon Point and at the entrance of Orcott Bay. Reids Rock, located at the mouth of the bay, is exposed above the lake surface and clearly visible. These hazards are marked by spar buoys and an unlit can "U5."

Lying in the middle of the lake between Diamond Point and Long Island are the privately owned Little and Big Canoe Islands. Rocky shallows extend to the north and south from the pair of islands. The limits of these shoals are marked by lit can buoy ("U3") to the north, and by unlit can buoy ("U4") to the south. Do not pass between these cans and the islands. These shoals are a Mecca for various species of fish, and serve as an excellent destination for both anglers and divers.

Several areas in this region of the lake have been designated as 5 mph zones. These include Green Harbor; Still Bay, between Cooper and Cannon Points; Orcott Bay; and Reids Rock north to the Diamond Point community beach.

Canoe Islands

Originally called Three Sisters Islands, Big and Little Canoe Islands received their present name back in 1875 when the American Canoe Association was founded here. They kept the headquarters there until 1925 when it moved to the mainland. Today the American Canoe Association is headquartered in Fredericksburg, Virginia, and has over 50,000 members. Little Canoe is now privately owned and has a small summerhouse on it. Big Canoe is owned by Canoe Island Lodge and is kept for exclusive use by their guests.

U3

CANOE ISLAND

SHALLOW
(Do not pass)

Little Canoe Island

SHALLOW

Big Canoe Island

0 ft.   250 ft.   500 ft.

Scale of Feet

SHALLOW
(Do not pass)

127   U4

▌ Marinas, Docking and Anchoring

Several excellent marinas are located in the Diamond Point area.

● Just to the north, **_Gilchrist Marina and Motel_** (518-668-5848) has been a fixture on Lake George for over 50 years. Gilchrist's has transient dockage as well as dockage for their motel guests, a boat launch, restrooms, and a store with bait, camping supplies, firewood, and some groceries. They also offer Lake George boat registrations, emergency towing, and boat rentals including pontoon boats, and V-hull powerboats.

● In Middleworth Bay to the north, **_Yankee Boating Center_**(518-668-5696) provides gas, pump out, repairs, a store with boating supplies, restrooms, and Lake George boat registrations. They also have a large selection of boat rentals including sailboats, powerboats, pontoon boats, and water sports equipment.

● **_Beckley's Boats_** (518-668-5225) is located on the north side of Middleworth Bay and can provide gas, Lake George boat registrations., porta-johns, and boat launching facilities. Parking for island campers and water taxi.

● The **_Lake George Club_** (518-668-5734) is located along the west shore just north of Middleworth Bay. This yacht club was established on November 16, 1908, and at the time, its membership represented the who's-who of Lake George Society. Today, The Lake George Club is still private with 300 members, and has a substantial waiting list of those wishing to join. The colorful sails of their regatta boats can be seen most weekends. Please be courteous when navigating in the vicinity of these regattas, and use care not to impede the racing sailboats. The Lake George Club marina facilities are available to members only.

Dockage is widely available in the vicinity of Diamond Point if you are staying at one of the many hotels, motels, and cottages in this area. Almost all of them provide dockage as part of your room rental, or for an additional fee. Public docks are located at the Diamond Point beach just north of Gilchrist Marina. However, these are pedestrian docks only — boats are not allowed to tie up.

Good anchoring sites in this area of the lake are limited due to the prevalence of relatively deep water and exposure to the open lake. However, good holding can be found in the vicinity of the Diamond Point public docks, south to Reid's Rock. Exercise caution and show courtesy to your fellow boaters if you choose to anchor here, since this is a busy area with two marinas, several resorts, and buoyed exclusion zones for swimmers along the shore. Also remember to obey the 200' limit for anchoring offshore of private property.

For snorklers and anglers, another favored anchorage is around the rocky shallows found at the north and south ends of the Canoe Islands. Getting a good hold in these areas can be tricky, so be sure your anchor is set if you plan to leave the boat to swim or snorkel.

▌Ashore

Lodging

Lodging is plentiful in the vicinity of Diamond Point. Working from south to north along the west shore:

● ***Cramers Point Motel & Cottages*** (518-668-2292) has cottages and motel rooms, pools, rowboats and canoes, and small beach a short walk from the motel. No dockage available.

● Just over a quarter mile north in Still Bay, ***O'Connors Resort Cottages*** (518-668-3367) offers cottages, suites, motel rooms, a private beach, rowboats, playground, and mini-golf.

● ***Still Bay Resort*** (518-668-2584) provides 22 rooms, sandy beach and docking for guests.

● Next door, the ***Depe Dene Resort*** (518-668-2788) offers motel rooms, beach suites, cottages, townhouses, and numerous amenities including expansive beach, paddleboats, rowboats, and dockage for their guests. The centerpiece of the Depe Dene resort is the large yellow mansion set on the hill overlooking Still Bay. The mansion is also available to rent.

Sailboats at sunrise near the Bolton town beach. Photo by Carl Heilman II

● Further north in Diamond Point, the *Diamond Cove Cottages* (518-668-3161) offer cottages, cabins, a spa, fitness room, kayaks, rowboats, private beach, and dockage for guests.

● *Golden Sands Resort* (518-668-2203), offers motel rooms, a large beach, playgrounds kayaks, and dockage for boats up to 18 feet in length.

● *Mt. Knoll Beach Cottages* (518-668-4875) and adjacent *Blue Lagoon Resort* (518-668-4867) each offer numerous amenities including lakeside beach settings and dockage for their guests. The Blue Lagoon has launching facilities. The Blue Lagoon has launching facilities, and sells fishing licenses and boat registrations.

● Continuing north, *Lake George Suites* (518-644-9633) offers suites, a beach house, large sandy beach, heated pool, and numerous other amenities.

● The *Gilchrist Motel* (518-668-5848) has motel rooms, boat rentals, dockage, launching facilities, and a full service marina.

● The *Stepping Stones Resort* (518-668-5532) is located along the water's edge north of the Diamond Point public docks. The Stepping Stones offers 2 & 3 bedroom cottages, volleyball, a large sandy beach, rowboats, ample dockage and launching facilities.

● The Adjacent *Olympian Village Motel* (668-668-5405) offers 40 rooms, sandy beach, large pool, rec room, and dockage for guests.

● Continuing north, the *Canoe Island Lodge* (518-668-5592) offers dockage, sailboats, cruise boats, tennis courts and a sandy beach. Their own private island, known as Big Canoe Island, lies approximately ¾ of a mile off the west shore (see sidebar on page 126). Today, the island is used exclusively by guests of the Canoe Island Lodge.

● A quarter mile north is the *Juliana Resort* (518-668-5191), with accommodations including motel rooms, cottages, and studios. They also have a heated pool, sandy beach, kayaks, a basketball court and boat dockage for guests.

● Further north, in Middleworth Bay, several more lodging options are available. The *Thunderbird Resort & Marina* (518-668-4824) has motel rooms, apartments, and cottages, plus numerous amenities including private beach, water sports, boat and jet-ski rentals, rowboats, and dockage for guests.

● The *Flamingo Resort* (518-668-5052) has over 50 rooms and numerous amenities including charter fishing, pools, private beach, volleyball, and dockage for guests.

● Just north, the *Capri Village* (518-668-4829) has 64 rooms, heated pool, game room, rowboats, kayaks, sandy beach, and dockage for guests.

● *Beckleys Lakeside Log Cabins* (518-858-9899) offers several waterside rustic cottages. Beckleys marina and boat launch are located nearby.

● *Treasure Cove* (518-668-5334) has two to five bedroom units, fireplaces, heated pools, paddleboats and rowboats, sandy beach, boat launch and docks.

Dining

Situated between Lake George Village and Bolton Landing, numerous dock and dine options are available within a relatively short boat ride. In the vicinity of Diamond Point you will find the *Diamond Point Grill,* serving breakfast, lunch and dinner in a family-style atmosphere. For great sandwiches and other supplies go to the *Pot Beli Deli* a few doors south. Both are located on the west side of Lake Shore Drive (Route 9). Several of the Diamond Point resorts also include dining facilities. You may want to inquire when making reservations.

Entertainment and Attractions

Diamond Point is only a few miles from the attractions of Lake George Village to the south, and Bolton Landing five miles north. In Diamond Point, *Lake George Island Adventures* (518-885-3838), run by Captain Justin Mahoney, offers tubing, swimming, and guided charters to several of the more popular islands. Captain Mahoney also runs *Highliner Fishing Charters* (518-885-3838) providing fishing excursions on board the 24' *Reel Comfort.* Several other fishing charter companies also operate out of Diamond Point including *Rod Bender Charters* (518-668-5657), *Lockhart Charters* (1-888-848-5253), and *Hooker Charters* (518-288-6668).

View over Lake George from Buck Mountain, looking to Northwest Bay and the Narrows. Photo by Carl Heilman II

Bolton and Vicinity

During both the French and Indian War and the American Revolution, the shores of Bolton on the west shore of Lake George served as a stopping-off point for British, French, and American troops traveling up and down the lake. After the wars settlers began trickling into the area, drawn largely by the availability of waterpower and vast forests of standing timber. Bolton was formally established in 1799, and within a short period began attracting tourists with George Washington, Thomas Jefferson, and James Fenimore Cooper among the most notable. Also known as Bolton Landing, this name actually refers to the hamlet surrounding Bolton's post office, established in 1882. The Mohican House was the first tavern and inn to operate in Bolton Landing, opened by Roger Edgecomb in 1802 on Mohican Point. Many other hotels would soon follow.

Bolton Bay looking south. Photo by Scott Padeni

Bolton

Today, Bolton is perhaps the best-kept secret of Lake George. Although often overshadowed by the bustle of Lake George Village, Bolton offers a wide range of fine dining, lodging, shopping, and entertainment at a more relaxed pace. Often referred to as the "Gateway to the Narrows," Bolton is situated at one of the most scenic locations on the lake, providing spectacular views. Moreover, the centralized location of Bolton offers the best of all worlds for the boater wishing to explore all points of the lake. For those camping on one of the many available islands in the narrows, Bolton makes a perfect staging area, with numerous marinas, launching facilities, and stores offering groceries and camping supplies. Further information on Bolton and what it has to offer can be found at the Bolton Chamber of Commerce website (www.boltonchamber.com).

Bolton Landing and vicinity map key

1. Diamond Village Resort
2. Chelka Lodge
3. Porters Cottages
4. Famiglia's Italian Deli
5. Cool-Ledge Resort
6. Blue Water Manor & Tavern on the Lake
7. Melody Manor & Villa Napoli
8. Red Gate Cottages
9. Northward Ho' Resort
10. Bonnie View on Lake George
11. Bay View Marina & Suites
12. Algonquin Restaurant
13. Chic's Marina Bay & Para-sail Sunsports Unlimited
14. Sembrich Museum
15. Point Motel
16. Twin Bay Village
17. Carey's Lakeside

18. Public & Steamboat Dock
19. Rogers Memorial Park
20. Public Parking
21. Bolton Historical Museum
22. Lakeside Lodge & Grille and Brass Ring Lounge
23. Performance Marine
24. Bolton Landing Marina
25. Frederick's Restaurant
26. F.R. Smith and Sons Marina
27. Boathouse B&B
28. Waters Edge Marina
29. Norowal Marina 🄸
30. Sagamore Resort
31. Lake George Kayak Company
32. Lake George Camping Co.& Marina
33. Veterans Memorial Park
34. Huddle Bay Beach & Public Dock

🄸 Inspection station

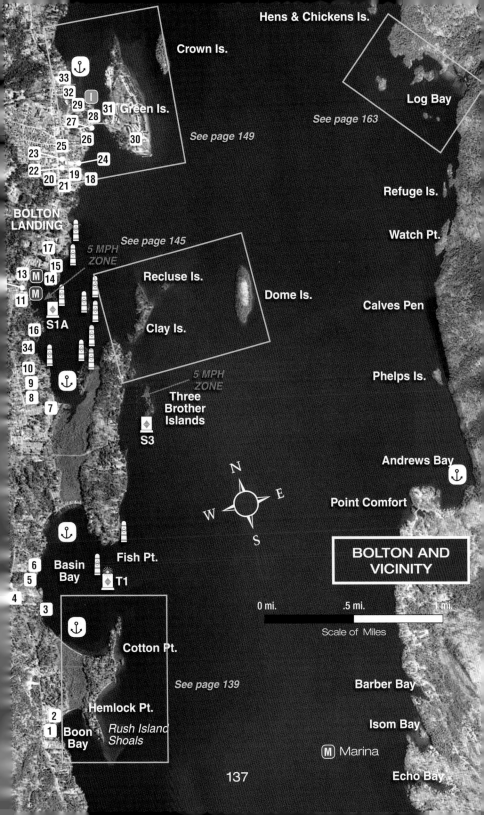

Hens & Chickens Is.

Crown Is.

Log Bay

See page 163

33
32
29
31 Green Is.
28
27
26
30
See page 149

Refuge Is.

23
25
24
22
19
20 21 18

Watch Pt.

BOLTON
LANDING

See page 145

17
5 MPH ZONE
15
13 M 14
11 M

Recluse Is.

Dome Is.

Calves Pen

S1A

16 Clay Is.

34

10
9 Three
8 Brother
7 Islands
S3

Phelps Is.

5 MPH ZONE

Andrews Bay

N
W E
S

Point Comfort

Basin Bay Fish Pt.

BOLTON AND
VICINITY

6
5 T1

4

3

0 mi.   .5 mi.   1 mi.

Scale of Miles

Cotton Pt.

See page 139

Barber Bay

2
1 Boon
Bay Hemlock Pt.
Rush Island Shoals

Isom Bay

M Marina

Echo Bay

Boon and Basin Bays

∎ Navigation

Basin and Boon Bays are situated in the southern portion of Bolton and north of Diamond Point. When navigating these bays there are several shoals to be avoided around Diamond Point at the mouths of Boon and Basin Bays. Rocky shoals ring the southern tip of Diamond Point around Rush Island. Today, the rocky outcropping is an island in name only, as Rush Island has been lost to erosion and ice, despite efforts by local residents and the state. The shoals at this location are marked by a ring of spars and can buoys marked "T3," "T4," "T5" and "T6." Can "T4" is a lighted buoy.

Remember not to pass between these buoys or between the buoys and the adjacent shoreline. Approximately one half mile north, shoals can also be found on the north and south sides of Cotton Island which are marked by spars.

Beware of Cotton Point shoal lying just below the surface about 350 feet east of Cotton Point's northern end. This rocky shoal is a favorite among divers who often find props, out-drives, and other boat parts left by the unwary boater. The shoal is marked by spar buoys and lighted can "T2."

Be sure to leave plenty of room between you and this shoal when passing between it and Cotton Point. Several obstructions are also marked along the west shore of Cotton Point on the Basin Bay side.

Another large submerged obstruction is marked nearly dead center at the mouth of Basin Bay between Cotton Point and Fish Point to the north. This rocky shoal rises up to only a couple of feet below the lake surface and is marked by spars and lighted can buoy "T1." This pinnacle-like shoal is also a favorite among divers and anglers.

At the north entrance to Basin Bay, a single spar marks a submerged obstruction found on the east side of Fish Point.

RUSH ISLAND SHOALS

Basin Bay

Cotton Point

T2

PRIVATE PROPERTY

Cotton Is.

Hemlock Point

T4

T3

Boon Bay

T5

SHALLOW (do not pass)

Rush Island Shoals

T6

N
W   E
S

Rush Is.

139

0 ft.   500 ft.   1000 ft.

Scale of Feet

▮ Marinas, Docking, and Anchoring

Marinas can be found south in Diamond Point or just north in Bolton Landing. No public docking is available in Boon or Basin Bays but several of the businesses in this area offer dockage to their customers.

There are several anchoring options in this part of the lake. Boon Bay offers protection from all but a southerly wind. If lake conditions permit, anchoring is also possible off the east shore of Cotton Point in the shallows south of Cotton Island. If anchoring here stay clear of the shoals previously described in this area. Some of the best anchoring can be found in Basin Bay, where sandy shallows can be found in both the north and south ends. It is not uncommon to see numerous boats anchored in these areas to swim or lounge during hot summer days.

Remember to not anchor closer than 200' from private property. This includes the southern shore of Basin Bay. Although wooded, this shoreline is privately owned — going ashore is prohibited.

▮ Ashore

Lodging

- In Boon Bay, *Chelka Lodge* (518-668-4677) offers a beach, dockage, for guests and seasonal boat owners, powerboat rentals, kayaks, rowboats, canoes, and numerous other amenities.

- The *Diamond Village Resort* (518-668-4689) is also located in Boon Bay and offers motel rooms or cottages, with a beach on the bay. They also have docks and launching facilities for their guests.

- On the north side of Diamond point in larger Basin Bay there are also several excellent places to stay. *Porters Cottages* (518-644-3018) provides immaculate cottages, fireplaces, a private beach, rowboats, canoes, kayaks, and deep-water dockage for their guests. Just ask for Joe.

- Further north in Basin Bay, the *Cool-Ledge Resort* (518-644-2211) also provides ample dockage for their guests, tennis courts, as well as a private beach with swim platform.

● The *Blue Water Manor* (518-644-2535) on Basin Bay has 70 cottages, and offers moorings and dockage and a private beach. Their amenities also include a restaurant, water skiing lessons, tubing, banana boat rides, an indoor heated pool, and game room for the kids.

Dining

● The *Tavern on the Lake* at *Blue Water Manor* (518-644-5400) This restaurant is a classic Adirondack Lodge built on a high ledge overlooking Basin Bay, providing spectacular views of the lake. Breakfast, lunch and dinner is offered throughout the summer and is open to the public. Live music is featured most nights in season. Deep-water dockage is available for patrons, but get there early as it fills up quick.

Ahoy Mates! Famiglia's Italian Deli

While on shore please visit Famiglia's Italian Deli located just 7 miles north of Lake George Village at 4375 Lakeshore Dr. (Rt. 9N), Diamond Pt., NY. (518) 668-0249. Custom cut steaks, burgers, chicken, and more. All salads, prepared foods and sandwiches are made on the premises

● If you are looking for sandwiches for the boat or excellent food to take back to your cottage, *Famiglia's Italian Deli* (518-668-2042) is located near Basin Bay on Lake Shore Drive across the road from Blue Water Manor and Porters Cottages. Famiglia's also sells groceries, a wide range of salads, firewood, and camping supplies.

Entertainment and Attractions

Situated between Bolton Landing and Lake George Village, there are an abundance of activities and entertainment options available whether going by boat or by car. In Basin Bay the Tavern on the Lake offers live music and dancing until the wee hours.

View from Blue Water Manor looking southeast. Photo by Peggy Huckel

The "Huddle"

Situated along the south shore of Huddle Bay is the hamlet known as the "Huddle." Among the earliest settlements in Bolton, it received its name around 1816 based on the mills, businesses, and homes that were "huddled" together at the mouth of Huddle Brook. Today, Huddle Bay is home to numerous private residences, marinas, restaurants, and resorts. The bay is bounded by Homer Point to the south, to the east by Clay Island, and to the north by Bolton Bay. Several islands are located in Huddle Bay, including Clay, Leontine, Hiawatha, Recluse, and Sweetbriar. Several other islands are located just east of Huddle Bay including Three Brother Islands, Dome Island, and Recluse Island. With the exception of tiny Sweetbriar Island, all of these islands are privately owned. Dome Island serves as a nature preserve and visitor access is prohibited.

▮ Navigation

Several shoals and channels are located in the vicinity of Huddle Bay. When approaching from the south, shoals can be found at the southernmost tip of the Three Brother Island. These shoals are marked by can buoy "S3." Shoals are also found at the north end of Three Brother Islands.

The southern access into Huddle Bay is through the narrow channel that lies between the mainland and Clay Island. This channel is known as the Gut and is marked by red and green can buoys "47" and "48." As the name implies, the passage is only about 20 feet wide and flanked by rocky shallows on either side. It allows passage for a single vessel only, and little room for error. Depth through the channel averages around 5 feet, so deeper draft vessels may want to consider using the northern route in or out of Huddle Bay. In addition, up

Dome Island

Dome Island lies about a half mile east of Huddle Bay. During the French and Indian War, Dome Island served as a lookout due to its elevation and location at the mouth of the narrows. In 1956, the island was donated by conservationist John Apperson to the Nature Conservancy. Now protected as a nature preserve and managed jointly by the not-for-profit groups Nature Conservancy and the Lake George Land Conservancy, visitor access to Dome Island is prohibited.

to 180 boats per hour use this channel during peak season, so line up your approach well in advance, slow down, and be sure the channel is clear of other vessels before attempting to navigate it. A 5 mph zone is in place on both sides of the Clay Island Channel. Once in Huddle Bay on this route, beware of shoals just to the northwest marked by can "S1" and lighted can "S2."

To the north, red and green can buoys "46" and "45" mark a second channel between Recluse and Clay Islands. Just northwest of this channel at the north end of Clay Island is a shoal area marked by spars and lighted can buoy "S."

Numerous shoals are located inside Huddle Bay, most of which are situated near Hiawatha, Leontine, and Sweetbriar Islands. Each is clearly marked. Be particularly careful not to pass between Sweetbriar Island and can buoy "S1A." Spar buoys off Mohican Point just north of Huddle Bay also mark shoals.

Gull Rock Shoal is an isolated shoal located between Recluse and the north end of Dome Island. Spars and lighted can buoy "R3" mark this shoal. For deep-drafted vessels, be especially cautious in this area, for there are several unmarked rocky shallows in the vicinity northeast of Gull Rock and north of Dome Island. These shallow areas extend up to a half mile northeast of Dome Island. At low water, these shallows can be five feet below the lake surface. Larger vessels passing up or down the lake avoid this area by passing between Little Recluse Island and Gull Rock via Bolton Bay, or by passing well east of Dome Island.

▋ Marinas, Docking, and Anchoring

Two marinas are available in Huddle Bay.

● *Chic's Marina* (518-644-2170) is located on the northwest shore of the bay and offers pontoon, powerboat, and Wave Runner rentals, and boat storage and repair. Chic's also offers parasailing, as well as wake board and water-skiing school.

● Just to the south in Huddle Bay, *Bay View Marina & Suites* (518-644-9633). The Bay View offers transient dockage, lodging accommodations, repairs, and launching facilities for guests only. Winter storage is available.

In addition to the above-mentioned marinas, several Huddle Bay restaurants and hotels also offer transient dockage.

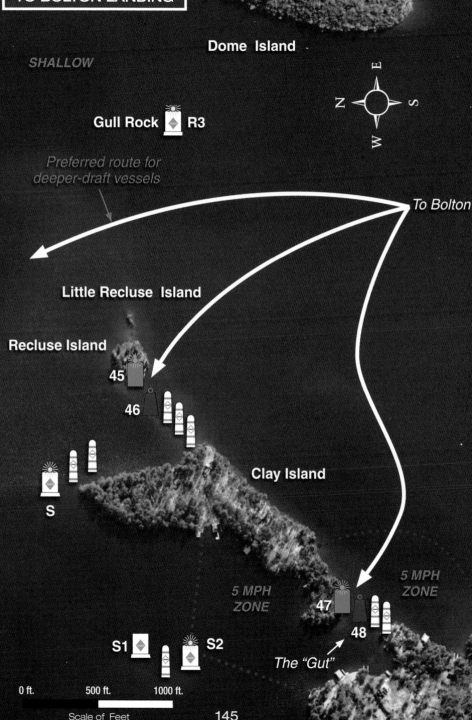

SOUTHERN ROUTES TO BOLTON LANDING

Dome Island

SHALLOW

Gull Rock ◆ R3

Preferred route for deeper-draft vessels

To Bolton

Little Recluse Island

Recluse Island

45

46

Clay Island

S

5 MPH ZONE

5 MPH ZONE

47

48

S1 ◆   ◆ **S2**

The "Gut"

0 ft.   500 ft.   1000 ft.

Scale of Feet

145

Huddle Bay is an excellent location for spending an afternoon at anchor fishing or just relaxing. Depths in the bay average 25 feet with a predominantly mud or sand bottom. The bay also provides protection from all but a north to northeast wind. Public dockage available at Huddle Bay Beach.

▌Ashore

Lodging

Several motels and resorts are located along the west shore of Huddle Bay.

● *Melody Manor* (518-644-9750) is situated at the south of the bay and offers dockage to their guests, a 300' sandy beach, heated pool, rowboats, basketball court, and numerous other amenities including their own restaurant, **Villa Napoli**. Melody Manor is located on the site of the William Becker Estate built between 1916-18. The 40-room mansion, named Villa Marie Antoinette for his wife, was torn down in 1953.

● A short distance north, *Red Gate Cottages* (518-644-5701) has 10 cottages, 250 feet of private beach and a limited number of docks for guests.

● Continuing north in Huddle Bay, *The Northward Ho' Resort* (518-644-2158) provides motel rooms and cottages, dockage for guests, and a sand beach. Other amenities include rowboats and swimming pool.

● Just next-door is *Bonnie View on Lake George* (518-644-5591). Bonnie View also offers both cottages and motel style rooms with ample dockage for your boat. Other amenities include a sandy beach, basketball court, rowboats and paddleboats.

● In addition to marine services, *Bay View Marina & Suites* (518-644-9633) rents several suites located on the marina grounds. Dockage for guests only.

● At the north end of Huddle Bay along the west shore you will find the *Point Motel* (518-644-2221), also providing cottages or motel rooms, dockage and private beach.

Dining, Entertainment and Attractions

While most dining and entertainment options are located just north in Bolton Landing, there are several excellent choices in Huddle Bay.

● Dock and dine options include the *Algonquin Restaurant* (518-644-9442), located on the west shore of Huddle Bay adjacent to Chic's Marina. The Algonquin offers both fine and casual dining indoors or on their large patio overlooking Huddle Bay. Free and ample dockage is available for their guests.

● At the southwest corner of Huddle Bay is the *Villa Napoli* (518-644-9750) on the grounds of the Melody Manor Resort. Proprietors Rose and Damian Alessi provide a taste of Italy with fine dining in the atmosphere of an Italian villa. Ten docks are available for restaurant guests. Use care when you make your approach, as their docks can be somewhat shallow with a sandy bottom.

● For entertainment or attractions in Huddle Bay, *Para-sail Sunsports Unlimited* (518-644-3470), based out of Chic's Marina, offers parasailing rides 300 feet above the lake. Powerboats, pontoon boats, and Wave Runners are available for rent at Chics Marina.

● For the opera enthusiast visit the *Sembrich Museum* (518-644-9839). The lakeside studio where famed opera singer Marcella Sembrich spent her summers is today a museum featuring opera memorabilia, including sculptures, personal items, photographs, music, and other items related to the "Golden Age of Opera."

Sagamore Resort. Photo by Peggy Huckel

Bolton Bay, Sawmill Bay, and Green Island

This area of the lake consists of two bays situated between the lake's west shore and Green Island. The northern bay is Sawmill Bay, and to the south is Bolton Bay. The two are divided by the Sagamore Road bridge spanning the narrow passage between Green Island and the mainland. Just east of Green Island is privately owned Crown Island.

▋ Navigation

During peak season, the waters of Bolton Bay, Sawmill Bay, and Green Island can be a hive of boating activity, with boat traffic second only to Lake George Village. Traffic is particularly heavy under the Sagamore Road bridge leading to Green Island as this narrow channel forms a bottleneck between Sawmill and Bolton Bays. Consequently, a 5 mph zone is designated in this area, which includes most of Sawmill Bay, continuing south approximately ¼ mile into Bolton Bay. This speed zone is strictly enforced. Vertical clearance under the Sagamore Road bridge is limited to approximately 7 feet above lake surface, so use care when passing under. Many a bimini top and VHF aerial have met their demise when passing under this low span.

Relatively few natural hazards to navigation are located in the vicinity of Bolton Landing. A few isolated shoals are buoyed along the west shore north and south of the Bolton Public docks in Bolton Bay. Shoals can also be found along the west shore of Green Island, just north of the Sagamore Bridge. When passing the north tip of Green Island, stay clear of a rocky shoal marked by spars and lighted can bouy "R2."

Along the west shore of Sawmill Bay, a large area of sand and mud shallows is located just offshore of Veterans Memorial Park, extending just over a quarter mile north to the outlet of North Brook. These sandy shallows are clearly marked by spar buoys. Also in the vicinity of Veterans Memorial Park is a swim exclusion area located in front of the public beaches at Veterans Memorial Park. Another swim exclusion area is designated just off the public beaches located at Rogers Memorial Park near the Bolton Public Docks. Buoys marked with an orange diamond and orange cross identify these exclusion areas (see pages 44–46 and 218–219 for buoy information).

BOLTON AND SAWMILL BAYS

N
W   E
S

R2

Veterans
Memorial Park

Public
Docks

5 MPH
ZONE

Crown Island

Sawmill
Bay

Green
Island

M

M

Clearance
approx. 7 feet

Bolton
Bay

Sagamore
Resort

5 MPH
ZONE

gers
emorial Park

Cruise Boat
and Public Docks

Cruise
Boat Docks

0 ft.   500 ft.   1000 ft.

Scale of Feet

▌Anchoring, Docking, Mooring and Marinas

Docking and Anchoring

In addition to the transient dockage provided by the below-listed marinas, public dockage is also available in Bolton Landing. At Rogers Memorial Park located on the west shore of Bolton Bay, recently renovated public docks are located adjacent to the steamboat dock. Public dockage is also available at Veterans Memorial Park located a half mile north in Saw Mill Bay adjacent to the public beach. Both of these locations have public restrooms, barbeque grills, picnic tables, pavilions, public beaches, playgrounds, and basketball courts. Use care when making your approach to these docks, and stay clear of nearby swim exclusion areas. The docks are free of charge, but have a 3-hour time limit. No overnight dockage is allowed. Both dock facilities are within easy walking distance to Bolton Landing restaurants and shopping.

The relatively shallow depths and sand/mud bottom of Saw Mill Bay provide several suitable locations to anchor. The most common locations for dropping the hook are along the western shore of both bays; a favorite is the sandy delta at the outlet of North Brook north of Veterans Memorial Park. Just be sure to stay well clear of swim areas, and to not anchor within 200 feet of shore. Also avoid anchoring too close to the Sagamore Road bridge channel. The route under this bridge is a major thoroughfare connecting Bolton and Saw Mill Bays, and one of the busiest areas of the lake.

Marinas

Six marinas are located in Bolton and Sawmill Bays and within easy walking distance to Bolton restaurants and shops.

- In Bolton Bay, *Bolton Landing Marina* (518-644-3474) offers gas and pump-out for members and the public; a clubhouse, showers, and dry-stack storage.

- *Performance Marine* (518-644-3080.) just to the north specializes in high performance boats, offering Mercury and Mercruiser authorized boat repair service.

- *F.R. Smith and Sons Marina* (518-644-5181) is located on the west shore just south of the Sagamore Road bridge. Services include boat repair and parts, gasoline, a ship's store with boating supplies, beverages, basic groceries and snacks. Powerboat, pontoon boat, kayak, and canoe rentals available along with water taxi and classic wooden boat tours.

● On the north side of Sagamore Bridge on Sawmill Bay, you will find *Waters Edge Marina* (518-644-2511). Services at Waters Edge include boat rentals, private charters, and water taxi services. Their fuel dock offers both 87 and 93 octane fuel. They also have a deli with a menu including excellent sandwiches, burgers, soups, and hot dogs. Be sure to try one of their tasty breakfast sandwiches while relaxing on their boathouse deck. Waters Edge also offers cottages for rent.

● Continuing north, you find *Norowal Marina* (518-644-3741) providing boat launching services, a ships store with snacks and camping supplies, pump out, gasoline, washer and dryers, and restrooms with shower facilities. Registration for Lake George Island camping can also be completed here. **This is an offical inspection station.**

● Just north of Norowal Marina is the *Lake George Camping Company & Marina* (518-644-9941). This marina has launch facilities, parking, gas, as well as powerboat, pontoon, canoe, and rowboat rentals. They also offer repair service, and transient dockage. Towboat US on Lake George is based out of this location, providing towing and water taxi service.

∎ Ashore

Lodging
Ranging from lake cottages to four-star accommodations, several lodging options in Bolton Landing are available.

● At the south end of Bolton Bay is *Twin Bay Village* (518-644-9777), offering rustic cottages, suites and motel rooms. They also offer sandy beach, pool, ping-pong, and canoes.

● Just to the north, *Carey's Lakeside* (518-644-3091) provides motel rooms or cottages, ample dockage for guests, a private beach, and other amenities including grills, ping-pong, and shuffleboard.

● If you are looking for the elegance of an historic Adirondack Bed & Breakfast, the **Boathouse B&B** (518-644-2554) is located just south of the Sagamore Road bridge on Bolton Bay. This B&B has been featured in numerous travel magazines and offers guest rooms or suites overlooking the lake. They also offer private boat tours in their motor-launch *Miss Boathouse*, a custom-built mahogany 33' Hacker Craft Sport motorboat. Dockage is also available for the boats of Boathouse B&B guests. The Boathouse B&B was the previous home of millionaire and avid powerboat racer George Reis. In the 1930s Reis won several American Powerboat Association gold cups on Lake George in his boat *El Lagarto* (The Lizard). Today, *El Lagarto* is on display at the Adirondack Museum in Blue Mountain Lake.

● Without question the most elegant and historic of all resorts on Lake George is the **Sagamore Hotel** (518-644-9400) located on Green Island. The four-star, four-season hotel commands one of the most scenic locations on the lake. The Sagamore offers every amenity imaginable, includ-

History of the Sagamore Hotel

In the late 1800s hotel operator Myron O. Brown solicited investors with the hope of building an exclusive resort hotel on Lake George. With the financial backing of several local and New York City millionaires, he purchased Green Island and formed the Green Island Improvement Company, openING the Sagamore Hotel in 1883. As intended, the elegant and well-appointed resort attracted the well off and elite from around the world.

Only ten years later in 1893, a fire heavily damaged the structure. Undaunted, the owners vowed to rebuild the hotel, and by 1894 the Sagamore II was reopened. The Sagamore II boasted the addition of modern conveniences including Edison electric lights, elevators, telephones and a telegraph. Unfortunately the hotel burned again in 1914 on Easter Sunday.

For years the Sagamore languished as owners were hesitant to reinvest more into the seemingly ill-fated hotel, but the hotel was rebuilt and fully restored by 1930. Expansion and improvements continued until the hotel was closed in 1981. The hotel was purchased by new owners in 1983, refurbished and modernized to its present grandeur. Today, the Sagamore Hotel is a four star, four-season hotel and is listed on the National Register of Historic Places.

ing numerous restaurants, pools and spas, dockage, boat rentals, kayaks, and even their own 72-foot excursion vessel, the *Morgan*.

Dining

Several restaurants and other eateries are available in Bolton Landing that are dock-and-dine accessible, with many others available within short walking distance of the Bolton Landing public docks.

● Several dining choices are available at the **Sagamore Resort** on Green Island, all of which are accessible by boat. *La Bella Vita* offers fine Italian food in a smart casual atmosphere. For casual dining in and Adirondack camp setting, try *Mr. Brown's Pub*. Both the *Veranda Tea & Raw Bar* and *Caldwells Lobby Bar* offer light fare in a pub atmosphere. The Sagamore Resort's outdoor *Pavilion* restaurant is situated on an expansive covered deck providing spectacular views of the lake while you dine. If you are looking for a more upscale dining experience, you may want to try the *Club Grill Steakhouse* at the golf course. Reservations for the Sagamore Resort's restaurants are recommended — call (518) 743-6101. To make arrangements to use the Sagamore's docks, you must call hotel security at (518) 743-6226.

Boats on the lake. Photo by Peggy Huckel

● Another dock-and-dine eatery can be found just north of the Sagamore Road bridge at **Waters Edge Marina** (518-644-2511). Their Waters Edge Lakeside Deli has an excellent selection of subs, sandwiches and salads. Or you can enjoy breakfast or one of the deli's "dock dogs" for lunch on their deck. This deli is especially convenient for boaters camping on one of the many islands in the Narrows, as they also sell groceries, beverages, beer, ice, firewood, and other supplies.

Numerous other dining options are also available in the town's center along Lake Shore Drive, only a short walk from the Bolton Public Docks. Dock your boat, stretch your legs, and explore the many possibilities.

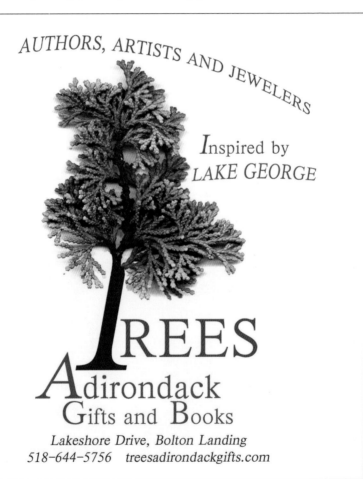

Entertainment, Attractions and Shopping

Since the late 1700s, people have been attracted to Bolton seeking the relaxation and escape that this quiet Adirondack town has to offer. Today, the attractions, shops, and entertainment found in Bolton continue to attract thousands of visitors each summer. Most are within a short walk of the Bolton public docks.

Live music can often be found on weekends and holidays at one or more of Bolton's restaurants and bars. At the **Lakeside Lodge & Grille**, live music is offered most Saturdays and holiday weekends in their **Brass Ring Lounge**, located in the lower level of the restaurant. **Frederick's Restaurant** also hosts live music on most weekends and summer holidays.

The Town of Bolton also provides regularly scheduled entertainment and events throughout the summer, including outdoor concerts, craft fairs, parades, festivals, theater and lecture series, and fireworks. Fireworks enjoyed from your boat offshore from Bolton are an event not to be missed.

Highlighted events for 2013 include:

May	Memorial Day Weekend Celebrations & Parade
June	Bolton Bikes & Bands
Jun–Aug	Sembrich Museum — Titans of Opera
June	Bolton Landing "Crossroads of the French & Indian Wars" military/nautical reenactment
June	North Country Triathlon (Hague)
Jun–Aug	Bolton Weekly Farmers Market
Jul–Aug	Free concerts in Rogers Park
July	4th of July Celebration including fireworks
July	Bolton Landing Emergency Squad Arts & Crafts Festival
July	Bolton Free Library Gigantic Book Sale
Aug	10th Annual Christine Nicole Perry Bike Ride
Aug	Bolton Landing Emergency Squad Arts & Crafts Festival
Aug	Chrissy's Chair Auction (conservation park)
Aug– Sep	Bolton Landing Emergency Squad Arts & Crafts Festival

Aug– Sep	Labor Day Weekend Celebrations & Fireworks
Sep	Bolton Landing Chamber of Commerce Annual Auction (The Sagamore)
Oct	Bolton Landing Emergency Squad Arts & Crafts Festival
Oct	Bolton Town Wide Garage Sale
Dec	Annual Christmas Tree Lighting

For further details and information on Bolton Landing scheduled events contact the Bolton Landing Chamber of Commerce at (518) 644-3831, or online at: www.boltonchamber.com.

Attractions in Bolton Landing include the ***ADK Adventure Course*** (518-494-7200), the ***Bolton Historical Museum,*** the ***Sembrich Opera Museum*** (518-644-2431) and **Sweet Pea Farm Gallery** (518-361-1995).

Sunset cruise on the Morgan. Photo by Peggy Huckel

At the **Sagamore Resort** on Green Island you can take advantage of Spas, world-class Golf, and lake excursions on the 72-foot excursion vessel *Morgan*. The *Lake George Kayak Company* (518-644-9366) located in Bolton on Green Island at 5 Boat House Lane in their beautifully restored 19th century boathouse. You can rent kayaks, stand up paddleboards, and canoes, take lessons, or take a guided tour on the lake.

As mentioned previously, Bolton Landing also boasts two parks with beaches that are boat accessible. Both the Rogers Memorial Park and Veteran's Park are open 7 am to 10 pm daily in the summer, and have sand beaches, restrooms, playgrounds, tennis courts, basketball courts, picnic tables and grills. When approaching the park's public docks, stay clear of the nearby swimming exclusion areas.

For those looking to shop, there's plenty in Bolton Landing within an easy walk from the public docks. Dispersed among Bolton's restaurants and ice cream shops on Lakeshore Drive in Bolton Center are a myriad of gift shops, galleries, antique stores, tackle shops, boutiques, wine and liquor stores, and flower shops. Groceries, camping supplies, and sandwiches can be purchased at Neuffer's Deli.

If you haven't already spent enough time on boats, Lake George Steamboat Company's excursion boats make daily stops at the Bolton public docks in Rogers Memorial Park. You can take a round-trip scenic cruise to Lake George Village, or ride back on the Lake George Trolley.

Boats on the lake off Bolton Landing, waiting for Fourth of July fireworks, photo courtesy Carl Heilman II

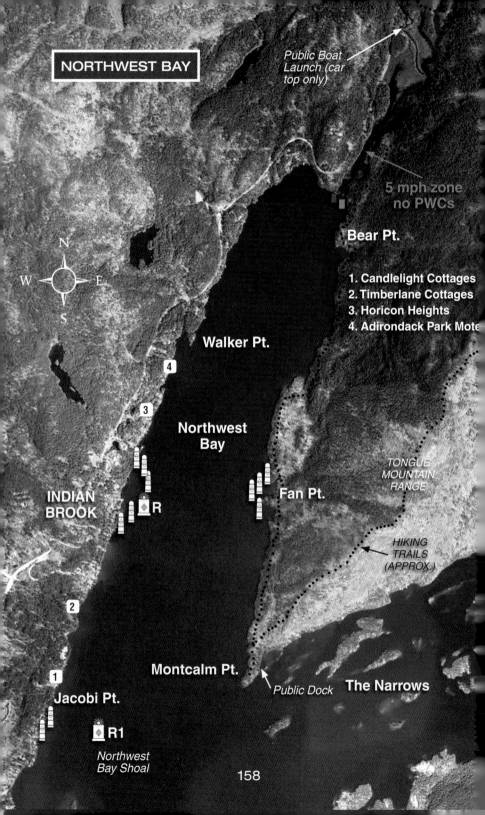

NORTHWEST BAY

Public Boat Launch (car top only)

5 mph zone no PWCs

Bear Pt.

1. Candlelight Cottages
2. Timberlane Cottages
3. Horicon Heights
4. Adirondack Park Motel

N
W — E
S

Walker Pt.

Northwest Bay

TONGUE MOUNTAIN RANGE

4

3

INDIAN BROOK R

Fan Pt.

HIKING TRAILS (APPROX.)

2

1

Montcalm Pt.

The Narrows

Public Dock

Jacobi Pt.

R1

Northwest Bay Shoal

Northwest Bay

Just north of Bolton Bay and approximately 12 miles from Lake George Village, the lake forks at the base of Tongue Mountain. To the northeast you enter the narrows and the main body of the lake leading to its outlet at Ticonderoga; to the northwest, you enter Northwest Bay. Northwest Bay extends just under three miles north, and is about a mile across at its widest point. As with much of the lake north of Bolton, Northwest Bay is lightly developed and is an excellent example of Lake George's pristine natural beauty.

▌ Navigation

Northwest Bay is generally deep and presents few hazards to navigation. Those hazards that do exist are clearly marked. Close to the center of the entrance to Northwest Bay lies Northwest Bay Shoal, several hundred yards north of Green Island. This isolated rocky shoal rises to only a few feet below the lake surface during low water and is marked by spars and lighted buoy "R1."

Spars mark another shoal just offshore from Jacobi Point along the west shore just north of Bolton Bay. Approximately 1¼ miles north of the Jacobi Point shoals is a very large sand delta situated at the outlet of Indian Brook along the west shore. These sand and gravel shallows extend several hundred feet offshore with depths often measured in inches. These shallows are delineated with spar buoys and lighted can "R." (Plans are in the works for the removal of this sand delta in the near future). Directly across Northwest Bay from the Indian Brook delta are rocky shoals near Fan Point at the base of Tongue Mountain. Several spar buoys mark these shoals.

At the north end of Northwest Bay you will find the narrow outlet of Northwest Bay Brook. This area of the lake is a kayaker's paradise, dominated by expansive wetlands, abundant wildlife, and breathtaking scenery.

Green and red buoys mark the channel leading to the Northwest Bay/Clay Meadow state boat launch. Depths through this channel are very shallow and only suitable for smaller, shallow-draft watercraft. The entire Northwest Bay Brook/Clay Meadow waterway north of the channel entrance is limited to 5 mph and off-limits to PWCs. The Northwest Bay/Clay Meadow boat launch is restricted to "car top" boats only, and is used primarily by kayakers and fishermen. The boat launch is free, has a small parking lot, and is located just over 4 miles north of Bolton landing off NY State Route 9N.

▌ Marinas, Docking and Anchoring

There are no marinas or public docks located in Northwest Bay. However, there are several marinas just to the south in Bolton Landing. Protected anchorages in Northwest Bay are also limited. Depending on wind and weather conditions, there are several small coves were you can drop anchor for lunch, a swim, or to just take a break and enjoy the view.

▌ Ashore

Lodging

● *Candlelight Cottages* (518-644-3321) offers cottages, large sandy beach, kayaks, rowboats, canoes, playground and dockage.

● *Timberlane Cottages* (518-644-5901) is also on the west shore of Northwest Bay and offers motel rooms and cottages, fireplaces, sandy beach, and dockage for guests.

● The *Adirondack Park Motel* (518-644-9800) is also on the west shore of Northwest Bay and offers motel rooms, efficiencies, cottages and a lake house. They also offer numerous amenities including a playground, kayaks, rowboats, canoes and dockage for guests.

Sunset over Montcalm Point, view west. Photo by Scott Padeni

● **_Horicon Heights_** (518-644-9440) is located on the west shore of Northwest Bay approximately three miles north of Bolton Landing. They offer cottages and a lake house, as well as sandy beach, playground, and dockage for guests.

Attractions

The biggest attraction in Northwest Bay, as with most of northern Lake George, is the location's natural beauty. As mentioned, Northwest Bay is one of the lake's more popular starting points for those wishing to kayak or canoe. Northwest Bay is also one of many stepping-off points for hikers seeking spectacular views from one of many mountain summits overlooking the lake. Trailheads for Tongue Mountain, French Point, and Fifth Peak are located just north of the Northwest Bay/Clay Meadow boat launch on Route 9. The Tongue Mountain trail is also accessible by boat at Montcalm Point. A state-owned boat dock for hikers is located on the north side of the point. You need a permit to use the dock, and it is first-come first-serve so get there early. Permits can be acquired at the Glen Island Ranger station.

Indigenous timber rattlesnakes are one of Tongue Mountain's claims to fame. These snakes pose little danger to hikers so long as basic precautions are followed. Wear high boots and always be aware of where you place your feet and hands. Also avoid stepping over large rocks or fallen logs where rattlesnakes may be sunning or hiding. Be aware that these animals should not be harmed, as they are an endangered species protected by law.

Phelps Island to Log Bay

This sparsely developed region of the lake lies along the east shore at the base of Buck and Shelving Rock Mountains. Some of the lake's deepest points are in this area, plummeting nearly 200 feet down off Watch Point. Moreover, it is not uncommon in this area to have depths drop precipitously just a short distance offshore. Several state owned islands are located here including Phelps, Refuge, Perch, Huckleberry, Log Bay, and Iroquois Islands.

▌Navigation

Due largely to the deeper water generally found in this area, navigation is relatively straightforward. However, several shoals do exist along the shoreline and surrounding a few of the islands. An exposed rock shoal approximately 330 feet south of Perch Island is marked by unlit can buoy "S5." Also use care when navigating near Perch and nearby Iroquois Islands. Rocky shallows can be found between the two islands.

Several shoals are marked in the vicinity of Log Bay Island. An elongated rocky shoal is located just south of Log Bay extending approximately 280 feet from the south side of the island. This shoal is marked by spars and unlighted can buoy "S4." At the north side of Log Bay Island, spars at the narrow passage between the island and the mainland mark another small shoal. Shoal waters are also found on the north side of Huckleberry Island.

Use great care when maneuvering in Log Bay and around its adjacent Islands.

Because of the shallow sandy bottom in Log Bay (Shelving Rock Bay), it is one of the more popular hangouts on the lake and can attract hundreds of boats on a sunny day. Be particularly cautious when passing between Log Bay Island and the mainland. This area is designated as a 5 mph zone. The northern route around Log Bay Island narrows to just over 100 feet, with a shoal along the island's north edge. In addition, there are numerous blind spots when using this route, so go slow and be prepared to avoid oncoming boat traffic. Many of the vessels here are often quite large, as camping on Log Bay Island is reserved for sleep-aboard cruisers. Also watch your fathometer, as depths here average around 5 feet.

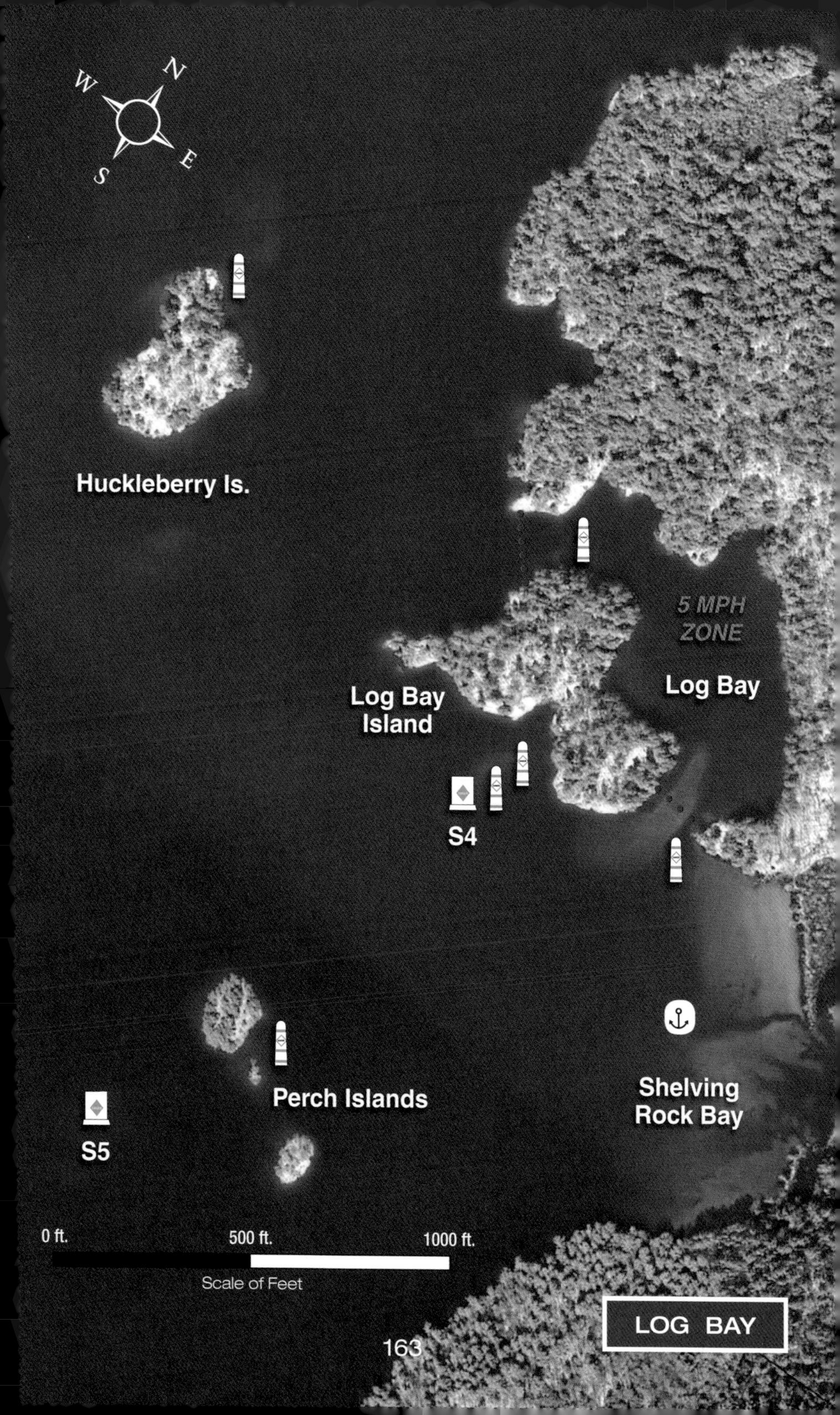

W N E S

Huckleberry Is.

5 MPH ZONE

Log Bay

Log Bay Island

S4

Shelving Rock Bay

Perch Islands

S5

0 ft. 500 ft. 1000 ft.

Scale of Feet

LOG BAY

▌Marinas, Docking and Anchoring

The closest marina in this area include ***Pilot Knob Marina*** (518-656-9211), located just to the south on the east shore. In addition, numerous marinas can be found just over two miles away to the west in Bolton Landing.

The only public docks available in this area of the lake are those docks that accompany island campsites. However, unless you have rented a site, do not tie up to campsite docks. The rightful occupants may not appreciate uninvited visitors occupying their rented dock space upon their return.

Suitable anchorages are somewhat limited due to the extreme depths found in this area. At many spots, depths in excess of 100 feet can be found just few feet off shore, which can be troublesome to the unwary boater. It is not uncommon for boaters to attempt anchoring near shore in what he or she assumes is shallow water, only to see their entire anchor and anchor rode disappear into the depths. Years ago in this area, I found six anchors in one dive, each with over 40 feet of attached line. Always be sure to secure the end of your anchor line to the boat prior to use.

One anchorage that is available in this area, however, is Log Bay (Shelving Rock Bay), a favorite among boaters on Lake George. The bay's sandy bottom

Canoeing in Northwest Bay. Photo by Carl Heilman II

and shallow water creates a natural playground for boaters wishing to drop the hook and spend an afternoon wading, socializing, sunbathing, grilling, or just watching the "wildlife." Because this anchorage is one of the most popular on the lake, it often attracts hundreds of boats on a good day, so use care when maneuvering here. When setting your anchor, be aware of nearby boats and leave plenty of swing room. You may want to hang fenders just as a precaution. Also be careful not to foul neighboring anchor lines.

Anchoring is also suitable two miles south in Andrews Bay where depths average around 40 feet. This anchorage can be rather uncomfortable in all but a southerly wind. As always, be respectful of local residents and do not anchor within 200 feet of private property.

▌Ashore

Lodging

Lodging in this portion of the lake is limited to camping on one of several state-owned islands. Though in many respects, camping gives you the best of both worlds by offering the seclusion of your own island retreat, with the dining, shopping and other amenities of Bolton Landing only a short boat ride across the lake. A total of 23 campsites are available on Phelps, Refuge, Perch, Huckleberry and Log Bay Islands. Each island site comes with its own boat dock. The 12 campsites on Log Bay Island are restricted to sleep-aboard cruisers, with no tents allowed.

View to the northeast from Cotton Point Road. Photo by Peggy Huckel

Entertainment and Attractions

Unquestionably, the greatest attraction on this portion of the lake is the natural beauty and solitude it offers. Days are spent boating, fishing, swimming, kayaking, and hiking, with evenings passed around a crackling campfire.

Several excellent hiking trails can be accessed from Log Bay. The Shelving Rock trail leads you to the summit of Shelving Rock Mountain and even includes a waterfall where you can stop to cool off. As with Lake George's rocky shoreline, use caution when negotiating the wet rocks of the falls, as slips can cause serious injuries.

One of the most popular Lake George "unofficial" events of the year is **Log Bay Day** held annually on the last Monday of July since 1997. Each year 400 to 500 boats anchor in the sandy shallows of the bay for one of the largest parties of the season. Festivities typically include live bands, water volleyball, dancing, and other assorted revelry. (Log Bay Day tends to be adult oriented, and is not recommended for children).

Scuba diving in this area of the lake is also popular. Many of the ledges and other geological formations make for excellent diving. Some of the best dive sites can be found along the east shore near Calves Pen, and off Refuge and Huckleberry Islands. Many of these dive sites are deep and should only be attempted by advanced divers.

Sailboat in late afternoon light on Lake George near Hague, looking south to Black Mountain. Photo by Carl Heilman II

The Narrows and Vicinity to the North End

Arguably, the most beautiful but dangerous region of Lake George is known as the Narrows. Beginning at Tongue Mountain Point and Fourteen Mile Island, the lake narrows to less than a mile across, hence its name. For over two miles northeast, the Narrows are dotted with numerous islands clustered closely together below the peaks of Tongue and Shelving Rock Mountains. These Islands are considered part of the Glen Island Group. With the exception of Oahu (Flora) and Fourteen Mile Islands, all are state owned and most are available for camping or day-use.

Approaching Paradise Bay. Photo by Scott Padeni

The Narrows and Vicinity

▌Navigation

Without question, the Narrows offers the greatest challenge to navigating on Lake George. Numerous shoals, shallows, and islets are strewn between the Islands creating a maze through which boaters must weave their way. The key to safely navigating this portion of the lake is to keep your speed down, and pay close attention to the numerous navigational buoys marking hazards. More often than not, boaters grounding in this area do so by failing to use marked channels, misjudging navigational lights at night, or by straying between grouped buoys marking one particular hazard.

When navigating the Narrows in a sailing vessel, it is advisable to do so under power or power sailing. Because of the adjacent peaks, winds in the Narrows can be erratic, with sudden and strong gusts typical. Also keep in mind: because of the restricted width of the marked channels through the Narrows, vessels under sail **do not** have right-of-way over any vessels restricted to that channel, such as the large excursion vessels that frequent these routes.

Rule 9: Inland Rules of the Road

A vessel of less than 20 meters (66 feet) in length or a sailing vessel shall not impede the passage of a vessel that can safely navigate only within a narrow channel or fairway.

At the southeast end of the Narrows, a series of shoals can be found just north of Hens and Chickens Islands and are marked by both can and spar buoys. A 5 mph zone exists in this area that includes the waters lying between Hen and Chickens Islands, Fourteen Mile Islands, and the mainland. This speed zone continues east to include all of Shelving Rock Bay.

Three major channels provide safe routes leading through the narrows. Lighted (flashing) red or green buoys mark the route of each channel. Always remember that when heading south on Lake George, or toward the "head of navigation," always keep the red channel markers on your starboard (right) side — RED, RIGHT, RETURNING, and the green buoys to your port (left) side. Also remember that red channel buoys, or nuns, are always evenly numbered, with green channel buoys, or cans, odd numbered. These numbers will decrease as you

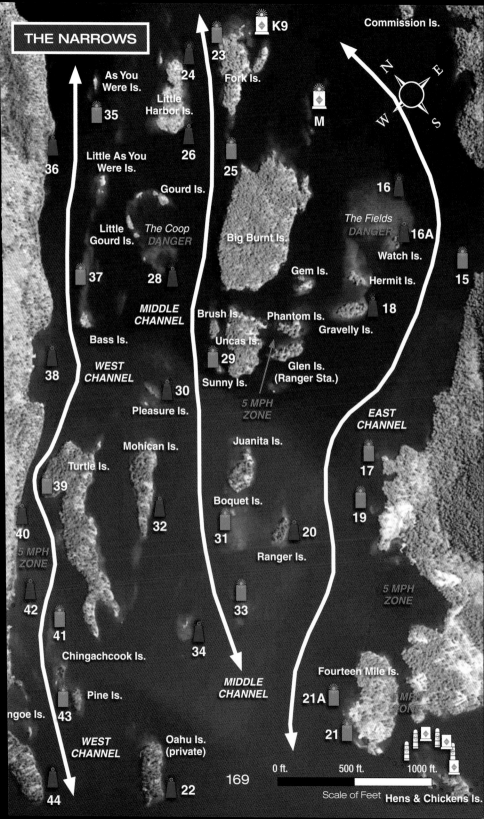

THE NARROWS

K9

Commission Is.

N
E
W
S

Fork Is.

23

24

As You
Were Is.

35

Little
Harbor Is.

26

25

M

Little As You
Were Is.

36

Gourd Is.

16

The Fields
DANGER

16A

Little
Gourd Is.

The Coop
DANGER

Watch Is.

Big Burnt Is.

37

28

Gem Is.

Hermit Is.

15

MIDDLE
CHANNEL

Brush Is.

Phantom Is.

18

Bass Is.

Uncas Is.

Gravelly Is.

WEST
CHANNEL

29

Glen Is.
(Ranger Sta.)

38

30

Sunny Is.

5 MPH
ZONE

Pleasure Is.

EAST
CHANNEL

Mohican Is.

Juanita Is.

17

Turtle Is.

39

Boquet Is.

19

32

31

20

40

Ranger Is.

5 MPH
ZONE

5 MPH
ZONE

42

33

41

5 MPH
ZONE

Chingachcook Is.

34

Fourteen Mile Is.

MIDDLE
CHANNEL

21A

Pine Is.

ngoe Is.

43

21

WEST
CHANNEL

Oahu Is.
(private)

169

22

44

0 ft.   500 ft.   1000 ft.

Scale of Feet   Hens & Chickens Is.

continue northeast, or away from the head of navigation. Never pass too close to any navigational buoy or channel marker, as their position may be approximate.

The first channel hugs the west shore of the lake along the base of Tongue Mountain. If headed northeast, red buoy "44" and green buoy "43" mark the channel's southern entrance at Tongue Mountain Point. Continuing northeast while staying between channel markers "40" and "39" you will pass Turtle Island to starboard. This section of the channel west of Turtle Island is designated as a 5 mph zone. With Turtle Island astern, leave red channel marker "38" well to port. Pass to the west of Bass Island and several marked shoals until you clear the channel between buoys "36"and "35." Personal Water Craft (PWCs) are limited to 5 mph when using this channel.

The middle channel through the Narrows is a straight shot and will bring you past the largest islands of the group, including Mohican, Uncas, Big Burnt, Little Harbor, and Fork Islands. When heading northeast into the Narrows using the middle channel, red nun buoy "34" and green can buoy "33" mark the channel's southern entrance. Keep between channel markers "32" and "31." Mohican Island will be to port, and Juanita Island will be to your starboard. Continue northeast between paired channel markers "30" and "29" leaving Sunny, Brush and Uncas Islands to starboard. The next channel marker will be red nun buoy "28" which you will leave to port as you pass Big Burnt Island to starboard. Just outside the channel to the west at this point, are numerous shoals including one of the more treacherous known as the "Coop." Be sure to stay in the marked channel and give it a wide berth. Proceed northeast between Little Harbor Island to port and Fork Island to starboard marked by buoys "24" and "23" which indicate the northern end of the channel. Be careful to avoid Black Rock Shoal approximately 600 feet northeast of the channel entrance. Personal Watercraft (PWCs) are limited to 5 mph when using this channel.

The third channel by which you can transit the Narrows is along the eastern shore of the lake. This is the easiest of the three routes and brings you past Fourteen Mile, Ranger, Glen, Gravelly, Hermit, and Watch Islands. This is also the only channel through the narrows that can be transited above 5 mph by Personal Watercraft (PWC's). The southern entrance to this channel is located just off the southwest tip of Fourteen Mile Island and marked by green can buoy "21" followed soon after by green can buoy "21A." Proceeding northeast, you will leave Ranger Island and red channel marker "20" to port. Clearing green channel markers "19" and "17" to your starboard, the channel turns almost due east after which you will leave Glen and Phantom Islands well to port. Continuing easterly you will pass red channel marker "18" to the west near Gravelly and Hermit Islands. With green channel marker "15"off your starboard side, make your turn northeast and leave red channel markers "16A" and "16" and Watch Island to port. This marks the northeast end of the channel.

When approaching the entrance to this channel from the north, favor the eastern shore of the lake, and remember to keep the red channel entrance marker well to starboard to avoid the numerous shoals that are located east and southeast of Big Burnt Island. A common occurrence for campers on Big Burnt Island is to hear the sound of boat out-drives scraping along the rocky shoals known as the "Fields," located just north of nearby Watch Island. Look for the numerous lighted hazard buoys and spars that mark this shoal and be sure not to pass between them.

Pine Island and Turtle Island in the Narrows. Photo by Peggy Huckel

Red Rock Point and Paradise Bay

In the vicinity of Red Rock Point northeast of the Narrows, several shoals are to be avoided. Marked by spar buoys, there are shoals found around the Commission Islands and near the east shore around Arrow Island. Some shoals are also buoyed along the west shore of Red Rock Point. Be particularly careful near Artist Rock as rocky shoals and shallows are located on all sides but the north of the small island. Most, but not all of these shoals are marked by can and spar buoys.

Red Rock Bay is one of the more popular locations on the lake for those with large cruisers since the campsites here are restricted to cruiser-use only. Due to often-heavy traffic and large cruisers, the entire bay is designated as a 5 mph zone.

Paradise Bay lies to the northeast of Red Rock Bay, separated by the narrow neck of land leading to Red Rock Point. Paradise Bay is one of the most frequented boater destinations on the entire lake and has been a favorite among boaters since the early 19th century. During the heyday of Millionaires Row, the lake's elite would often bring guests on steam driven yachts to Paradise Bay for afternoon tea or dinner. Today, it is not uncommon to find scores of boats lazily drifting in the well-protected bay. Two routes of access are available for those entering Paradise Bay. The southwest route takes you between Sarah Island and the mainland. When using this route, be wary of a submerged rock just off Sarah Island, near the mouth of the channel leading into the bay. A can buoy marks this hazard. The north route into Paradise Bay is via a narrow channel between Sarah Island and the mainland. This route is relatively deep and free of shoals. Depths in Paradise Bay average about 20 feet. Due to its popularity, the bay is often crowded. Take your time when entering or exiting the bay, and be ready to maneuver.

All of Paradise Bay is a restricted use zone. Special regulations apply and include:

- No anchoring or mooring within the zone between May 15 and September 15 except during emergencies.
- No "rafting" of vessels, and no tying to navigation buoys, to the shore, or to any object on shore.

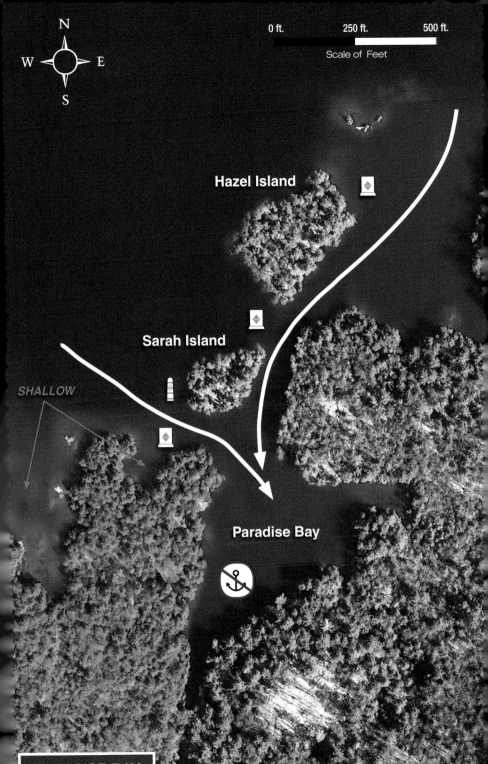

• No beaching of vessels.

• No vessels can be left unattended.

Source: Lake George Park Commission

▌Marinas, Docking and Anchoring

The nearest marinas are located southwest in Bolton Landing. Docking is available to those renting campsites. Dockage is also available with day-use sites by permit only. Day-use sites are located at Commission Point, and on Sarah and Hazel Islands. Day-use permits are available at the ranger station located on Glen Island in the Narrows. They can be contacted at (518) 644-9696.

Because of the numerous islands and protected coves, anchoring options in this region of the lake are plentiful. Favorite anchorages include Red Rock Bay and in the lee of Commission Point. Avoid anchoring in channels, or within 200 feet of private property. In addition, try to avoid anchoring at locations with rocky bottoms, since holding will be difficult, or worse, could result in a lost anchor. You may want to use a trip line on your anchor if a rocky bottom is suspected.

▌Ashore

Lodging, Activities, Attractions and Entertainment

Options for lodging in the Narrows are limited to camping, which is also this area's greatest attraction. There are 104 island sites and 36 mainland sites available for rent in the Narrows. Thirty of these sites, located at Red Rock Bay, are cruiser only. Reservations for sites in the Narrows book months in advance so be sure to call early with several back-up choices in mind. Reservations can be made up to nine months in advance. Information and links regarding camping and reservations can be found at www.lakegeorge. com/guide/island-camping.cfm

Hiking is also a favorite activity in the Narrows, allowing you to experience spectacular views of Lake George and nearby Lake Champlain from the peaks towering above the lake. Wildlife including beaver, deer, and bald eagles are commonly seen during hikes. Trailheads are located at Tongue Mountain Point, Commission Point, and Red Rock Bay. Docks are available by permit at each location.

Pack a lunch and enjoy the lake's natural beauty at one of several State picnicking sites located in the Narrows. Day-use picnic sites are available at Sarah and Hazel Islands. Use of these sites is by permit only. Permits can be acquired at Glen Island Ranger Station.

The numerous shoals and rocky ledges found in the Narrows make it an excellent location for snorkeling. A wide variety of fish can be found frequenting the rocky shallows.

Provisions, including groceries, ice, camping supplies, ice cream, firewood, coffee, and other items are available at **Neuffers Grocery** next to the Ranger Station located on Glen Island. You will also find public phones, and restrooms. Neuffers is open 8:00 am to 8:00 pm daily. Several short-term docks are available for patrons. Watch for the small stone lighthouse marking a shoal along the eastern approach to Glen Island.

Sailboat and the Narrows from the Sagamore dock. Photo by Carl Heilman II

French Point to
the Mother Bunch Islands

Between French Point and the Mother Bunch Islands is one of the most isolated regions of the Lake. Little development is found here with the exception
of the occasional summer residence. The steep rugged slopes of the Tongue
Mountain Range to the west, and Black Mountain to the east meet the water
along jagged shorelines to create a fiord-like atmosphere. This section of the
lake is home to numerous islands, most of which are state-owned and available to campers. Among these is a cluster of over 15 islands referred to as the
Mother Bunch Group. The Ranger Station on Glen Island in the Narrows
administers lands and islands south of, and including Black Mountain Point;
the Ranger Station on Narrow Island, near Huletts Landing, administers
state lands and islands to the north of Black Mountain Point.

▮ Navigation

While not as challenging as the Narrows to the south, navigating this region
of the lake can be tricky, as there are a large number of shoals and small islets
presenting hazards to the unwary. Several of these are isolated shoals located in
otherwise deep water well offshore.

A good example is a pair of shoals that straddle the lake east of French Point.
The first of these shoals is situated in the center of the lake and is marked by
lighted can buoy "K8." To the west of this shoal, and approximately one-quarter
mile east of French Point, is the second shoal, marked by lighted can "K5."

Just under a half-mile north of French Point, several shoals are to be
avoided near East and West Dollar Islands. Shoals just to the south and east
of these islands are marked by spars and unlighted can buoys "K2," "K3" and
"K4." Do not attempt to pass between East and West Dollar Islands, as the
route between the two is extremely shallow.

Across the lake on the east shore, spars or cans mark shoals that are particularly numerous northeast of Hazel Island, and continue for about a quarter
mile to Poppal Point. Among these is Fox Bay Shoal, marked by lighted can
buoy "K6."

Stay clear of several shoals just off Black Mountain Point, and of a particularly nasty isolated rock about a quarter mile north of Black Mountain Point,

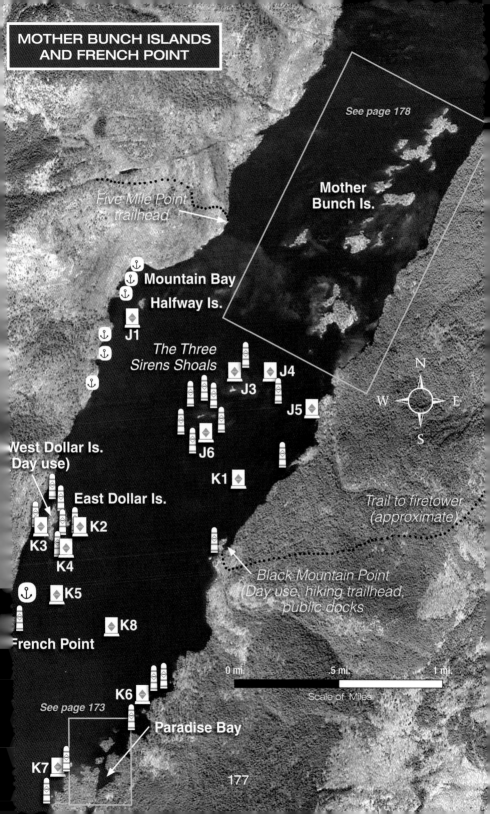

MOTHER BUNCH ISLANDS AND FRENCH POINT

See page 178

Mother Bunch Is.

Five Mile Point trailhead

Mountain Bay

Halfway Is.

J1

The Three Sirens Shoals

J4

J3

J5

J6

**West Dollar Is.
(Day use)**

K1

East Dollar Is.

K2

K3

K4

Trail to firetower (approximate)

K5

K8

Black Mountain Point (Day use, hiking trailhead, public docks

French Point

N

W   E

S

See page 173

K6

0 mi.   .5 mi.   1 mi.

Scale of Miles

Paradise Bay

K7

177

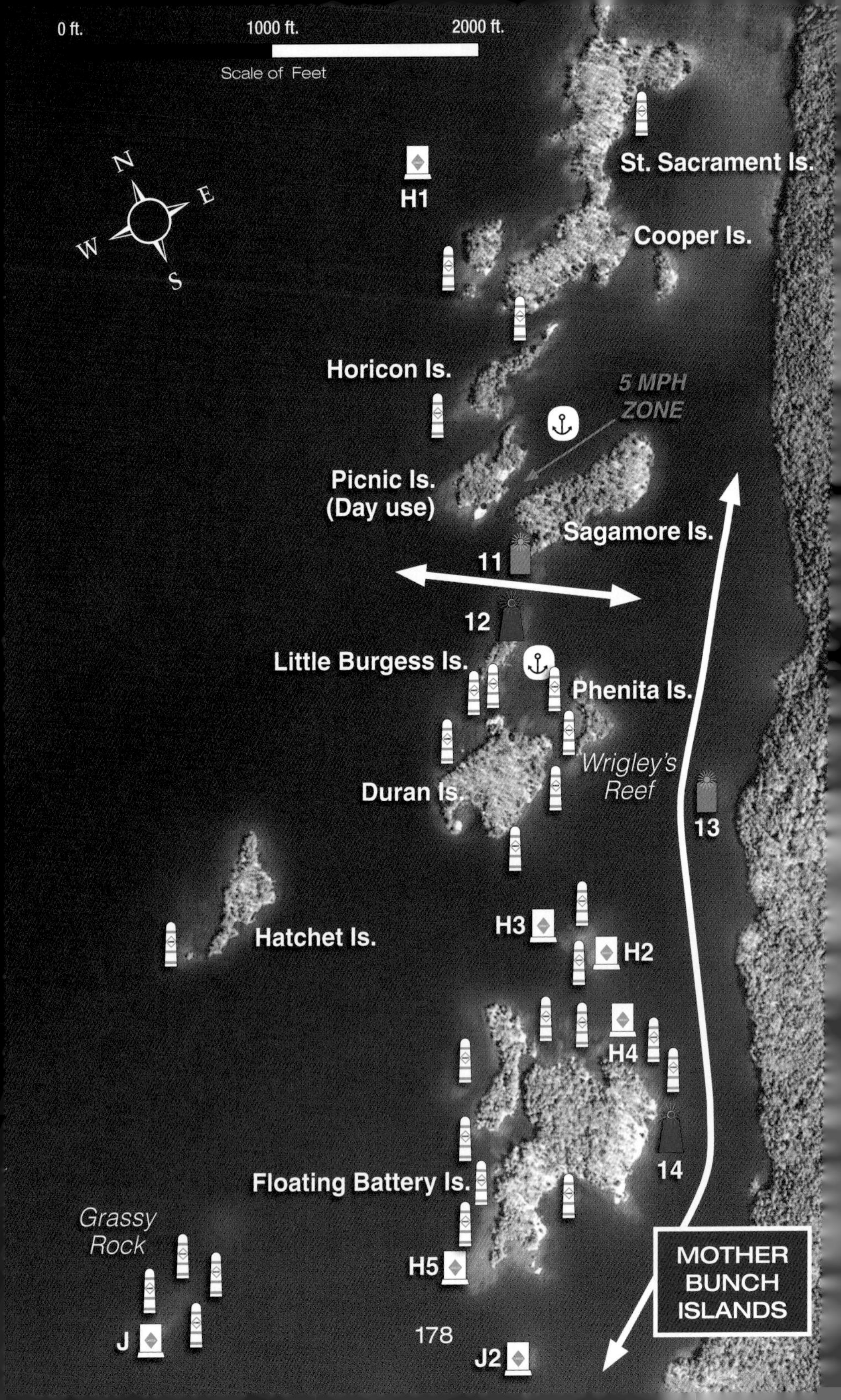
0 ft.
1000 ft.
2000 ft.
Scale of Feet
N
E
W
S
H1
St. Sacrament Is.
Cooper Is.
Horicon Is.
5 MPH
ZONE
Picnic Is.
(Day use)
Sagamore Is.
11
12
Little Burgess Is.
Phenita Is.
Wrigley's
Reef
Duran Is.
13
Hatchet Is.
H3
H2
H4
14
Floating Battery Is.
Grassy
Rock
H5
MOTHER
BUNCH
ISLANDS
J
J2

sitting approximately 530 feet off the east shore. This rock is marked by spars and lighted can buoy "K1."

At the center of the lake just over a half-mile north of Black Mountain Point, there is a large area of shoal water to be avoided. This area includes several small islands, known as the Three Sirens. The Three Sirens and surrounding shoals are marked by spars and unlighted can buoys. Another small rocky island, known as Fish Island, lies a quarter mile east and is marked by spars and unlighted can buoy "J4." Just over a quarter mile north of the Three Sirens is Grassy Rock, marked by spars and lighted can buoy "J."

An exposed rock is also marked 215 feet southwest of Halfway Island by unlighted can "J1."

The Mother Bunch group of islands is made up of 12 larger islands that include Floating Battery, Hatchet, Duran, Phenita, Little Burgess, Sagamore, Picnic, Horicon, St. Sacrament, Cooper, and Mother Bunch Islands. Distributed among these larger islands are numerous often-unnamed smaller islands and rocky shoals.

Use extreme care when maneuvering among these islands and be sure not to pass between obstruction buoys and shore, or between grouped buoys and/or cans marking a shoal.

Two channels are marked through this island grouping. The first follows the east shore of the lake passing east of Floating Battery, Duran, and Phenita Islands. The south end of this channel is marked by red lighted can buoy "14," with the north end marked by a green lighted can placed on Wrigley's Reef. The second channel provides a passage through the shallows between Little Burgess and Sagamore Islands. This narrow channel is marked by lighted red can "12" and lighted green can "11." The waters surrounding this channel are extremely shallow, so make your approach to the channel markers as close to a right angle as possible, while staying as near the center of the channel as practicable. Once through, maintain your course and speed until you are well and clear into deeper water.

Be sure to keep the red channel markers to starboard when traveling south, or to port when traveling north. A 5 mph speed zone is in place between the day-use Picnic Island and Sagamore Island.

Hemlock Shoal is an isolated shoal located just off the west shore, northwest of the Mother Bunch Islands and is marked by lighted can buoy "H."

▮ Marinas, Docking and Anchoring

The nearest marina is **Huletts Landing Marina** (518-499-0801) in Huletts Landing located several miles north. Huletts also has the nearest boat launch in this area of the lake. **This is an official inspection station.**

Public docking in this region of the lake is limited to campsite docks and day-use/picnic site docks. Day-use picnic sites with dockage are located on West Dollar Island, Picnic Island, and at Black Mountain Point. These docks are used by permit only. Permits can be obtained at the Glen Island Ranger station for West Dollar Island and Black Mountain Point; and for Picnic Island, permits can be acquired at the Narrow Island Ranger station near Huletts Landing.

Several of my favorite anchorages are found in this part of the lake. One of those is a small cove on the north side of French Mountain Point. This anchorage provides good holding in about 10-15 feet of water, protection from the prevailing winds, and spectacular views. Great snorkeling can also be found here around the old steamboat dock cribbing off the end of the point, and among the large submerged rocks along the west shore.

Excellent anchorages can also be found among the cluster of islands known as the Mother Bunch Group. A favorite location is in the atoll-like basin formed by Horicon, Picnic, and Sagamore Islands. This spot offers excellent holding in depths ranging between 10-25 feet. With islands on three sides, it also provides excellent protection from most winds, or from the occasional thunderstorm that may roll through.

Some tranquil anchorages can be found along the west shore near Halfway Island, Including Mountain Bay and several small coves to the south.

▮ Ashore

Lodging and Attractions
Hotels and cottages are available for rent several miles to the north in Huletts Landing.

Camping is also available on numerous state-owned islands. Sixty-one island campsites are available in this region of the lake on 13 islands including, Coop, Duran, East Dollar, Fox, Floating Battery, Hatchet, Horicon, Little Burgess, Phenita, Mother Bunch, Sagamore, and St. Sacrament. Fifteen campsites are also available along the east shoreline at the base of Black Mountain. All of these sites come with docks. Campsite docks at Coop, Sagamore, and St. Sacrament Islands tend to have deeper water and may be better suited for deeper drafted boats.

As with the Narrows to the south, picnicking, hiking, kayaking, fishing, snorkeling, swimming, and breathtaking views are the greatest attractions in this area of the lake.

Excellent **hiking** is available from boat-accessible trailheads located nearby. At Black Mountain Point, a trailhead leads you to a 3-mile hike up to the 2700-foot summit of Black Mountain. At the top, you will find stunning views of Lake George and Lake Champlain, and one of the few remaining fire towers in the Adirondacks. Other trails are also accessible from Black Mountain Point. Public dockage is available for hikers in the north bay of Black Mountain Point. A day-use permit is required. On the west side of the lake, a trailhead is boat accessible at Five-Mile Point, with trails leading to Five-Mile Mountain, and the entire Tongue Mountain Range. There are no docks available at the Five-Mile Point trailhead.

Several great locations for **snorkeling and scuba diving** can be found in this area of the lake. At the east tip of French Point submerged stone cribbing from a 19th-century steamboat dock is home to numerous species of fish and makes for a great dive with visibility reaching 50–60 feet. Excellent snorkeling and scuba diving can also be found along the lake's rocky west shore. In the small north bay of Black Mountain Point, divers will find the remains of the 1857 steamboat *Minne-Ha-Ha* lying about 30 feet north of the public docks in 15 feet of water. The 140-foot steamer was abandoned at Black Mountain Point and sank by the end of the 1890s. Because of nearby public docks, snorkeling this site is not possible during the summer season.

Day-use picnic sites are available at West Dollar and Picnic Islands, and at Black Mountain Point. Permits for West Dollar Island and Black Mountain Point can be acquired at Glen Island Ranger Station. Day-Use permits for Picnic Island can be acquired at Narrow Island near Huletts Landing.

Huletts Landing, Sabbath Day Point, and Vicinity

The small hamlets of Huletts Landing and Sabbath Day Point are situated on opposite shores roughly midway up the lake. Huletts Landing lies on the east shore nestled at the base of Elephant, Hogback and Spruce Mountains, and until modern times was accessible only by water. This tranquil community has a summer population of roughly 90 persons, and largely closes down during the winter months. The hamlet gets its name from the Hulett family that first settled here in the early 19th century. On the opposite side of the lake lies historic Sabbath Day Point and Silver Bay.

These picturesque Adirondack communities are comprised largely of private residences and summer homes. Amenities in this remote region of the lake are limited, though marina facilities, lodging, dining and other services are available.

▮ Navigation

This region of the lake is generally deep and relatively narrow, averaging less than a mile across. A number of islands are also found here, most of which are owned by the State and available to campers or picnickers.

With some notable exceptions, shoals in this portion of the lake are found close to the shoreline, or in association with islands. As always, be alert when operating near shore as not all of these shoals are marked.

A series of shoals and shoal waters surround the Harbor Island Group, which includes Eagle, Hecker, and Hewitt Islands. These hazards are marked by spars and unlighted can buoys. Be careful to avoid an isolated shoal located approximately 750 feet west of Hewitt Island. This shoal is roughly midway between the island and west shore, and is marked by lighted can "G4." The narrow passage between Hewitt and Hecker Islands, known as the *Needles Eye*, can be navigated by smaller vessels, but use care.

Two hazards known as Davis Bay Shoal and Seymour Shoal straddle the passage between Vicars Island and the west shore. Lighted can buoys mark each of these shoals. Numerous shoals are identified along the edge of the east shore from Huletts Landing to Mallory Point five miles north. Most are just off shore and marked by hazard buoys. Several more prominent shoals near Huletts Landing warrant special mention. If approaching Woodcock or Kitchell Bays in Huletts Landing, avoid Whale Rock Shoals located about 750 feet north of Nobles Island. Spars and lighted can buoys "F4" and "F5" mark these rocky outcroppings. Northwest of Hewitt Island is another isolated shoal marked by lighted can buoy "F3." Also stay clear of the shoal associated with Loon Island, located about 450 feet due west of Meadow Point.

If heading to the Ranger Station on Narrow Island, pay attention to the shallows between Narrow and Huletts Islands. Green and Red buoys mark the channel between the two islands. Be sure to keep the red buoy to starboard if approaching from the west toward Huletts Landing. A marked channel is also located on the east side of Narrow Island, allowing passage between Narrow Island and the mainland. This channel is not shown on available charts. Rocky shoals are also to be avoided along the north shore of Agnes Island. Heading north from Huletts Landing, an isolated shoal, known as Three Chimney Shoal, is located about a quarter mile due south of Sabbath Day Point and is marked by lighted can buoy "F1."

Along the west shore, extensive shoaling is found along the east shore of Sabbath Day Point, continuing a mile north to, and including, Bass Bay. Bass Bay is designated as a 5 mph zone. Another isolated shoal is located toward the center of the lake, approximately a quarter mile northeast of Sabbath Day Point. This hazard is marked by lighted can buoy "E7."

Continuing north, a large shoal extends east from the tip of Slim Point, near Silver Bay, to a point approximately 600 feet from shore. Spars mark the length of the shoal, with its eastern end marked by lighted can buoy "E1."

Do not pass between this can buoy and Slim Point.

Sabbath Day Point

Situated roughly halfway up the lake, Sabbath Day Point boasts a rich history. During both the French and Indian War and the American Revolution, this point of land often served as an encampment site for military forces of the Americans, British and French traveling up and down the lake. Notable visitors to Sabbath Day Point included Benjamin Franklin, Thomas Jefferson, Henry Knox, and George Washington.

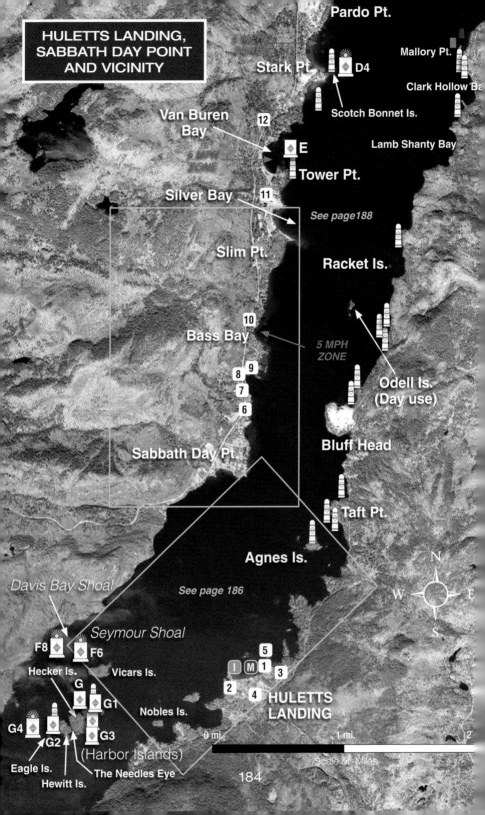

HULETTS LANDING, SABBATH DAY POINT AND VICINITY

Pardo Pt.

Mallory Pt.

Stark Pt.
D4

Clark Hollow Ba

Scotch Bonnet Is.

Van Buren Bay

12

Lamb Shanty Bay

E

Tower Pt.

Silver Bay

11

See page188

Slim Pt.

Racket Is.

5 MPH ZONE

Bass Bay

10

9

8

7

Odell Is.
(Day use)

6

Sabbath Day Pt.

Bluff Head

Taft Pt.

Agnes Is.

Davis Bay Shoal

See page 186

N

W   E

S

Seymour Shoal

F8
F6

5

Hecker Is.

Vicars Is.

I M 1

3

G

2

4

HULETTS LANDING

G1

Nobles Is.

G4
G2
G3

Eagle Is.

0 mi.

1 mi.

2

The Needles Eye

Hewitt Is.

(Harbor Islands)

Scale of Miles

184

Huletts Landing and vicinity map key

1. Huletts Landing Marina 🅘
2. Huletts-on-the-Lake Cottages and Casino Recreation Center
3. Huletts Park
4. Huletts Golf Course
5. Ranger Station (Narrows Island)
6. Northbrook Cottages
7. Snug Harbor South
8. Carol's Cozy Cottages
9. Morgan Marine
10. Northern Lake George Resort & Martucci's Restaurant
11. Silver Bay YMCA of the Adirondacks
12. Silver Bay General Store

🅘 Inspection station 🅜 Marina

At the mouth of Van Buren Bay, Cowhide Shoal extends approximately 350 feet north from Tower Point. This elongated shoal is marked by spars with an unlighted can buoy marking its outer end.

Avoid passing between the can and Tower Point.

Van Buren Bay is designated as a 5 mph zone. At Stark Point, just under a mile north, shoal waters surround several small islands just off shore. Least visible of these is Scotch Bonnet Island, lying 425 feet southeast of the tip of Stark Point. This rock is marked by a pair of lighted can buoys, both marked "D4," and one spar. Spars also mark shoals extending off the north end of Stark point. A short distance north, a 5-mph zone is marked along the south shore of Pardo Point.

Directly across the lake at Mallory Point, red and green channel markers provide a safe route past Mallory Island and shallows to the south. Be sure to stay between the red and green channel markers.

▮ Marinas, Docking and Anchoring

● *Huletts Landing Marina* (518-499-0801) is located in Huletts Landing. Huletts provides launch facilities, winter storage, restrooms, and canoe/kayak rentals. They also have a marina store with groceries, camping supplies, ice, beer, beverages, ice cream, and basic marine supplies.

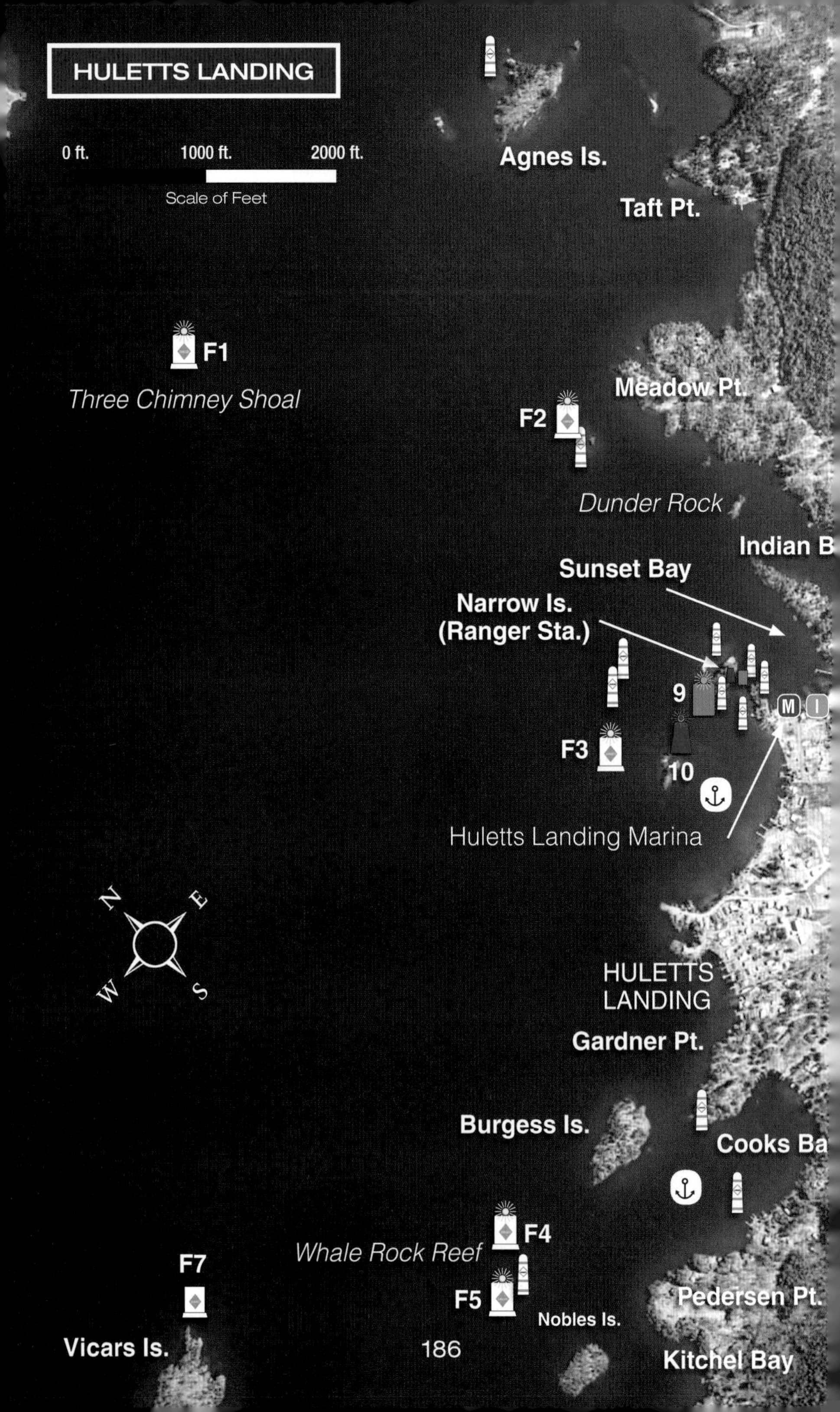

HULETTS LANDING

0 ft. 1000 ft. 2000 ft.

Scale of Feet

Agnes Is.

Taft Pt.

F1

Three Chimney Shoal

Meadow Pt.

F2

Dunder Rock

Indian B

Sunset Bay

Narrow Is.
(Ranger Sta.)

9

F3

10

Huletts Landing Marina

N
E
W
S

HULETTS
LANDING

Gardner Pt.

Burgess Is.

Cooks Ba

Pedersen Pt.

Whale Rock Reef **F4**

F7

F5

Nobles Is.

Vicars Is.

186

Kitchel Bay

● Just over three miles north on the west shore you will find ***Snug Harbor South*** (518-543-8866). Snug Harbor South offers power boat rentals. Their store carries campingsupplies, bait and tackle, groceries, and firewood.

● Just to the north is ***Morgan Marine*** (518-543-6666). Morgan Marine is a full-service marina providing gas, repairs, and emergency tow. Morgan is also the home of Hacker Boat Company, builder of Hacker-Craft boats.

Dockage is also available to patrons of several local restaurants, as well as to guests at most of the waterfront motels and resorts. Dockage is included with island campsite rentals, and there is a single public dock at the day-use picnic site on Odell Island. Short term docking is also available at the Ranger Station on Narrow Island for those making campsite arrangements. Washington County Beach at Huletts Landing has dockage available for launching canoes, kayaks, and smaller car top boats. No overnight docking allowed.

Huletts Landing. Photo by Peggy Huckel

SABBATH DAY POINT

SILVER BAY ASSOC.

Steamboat Dock

Silver Bay

0 ft.　1000 ft.　2000 ft.　3000 ft.

Scale of Feet

Slim Pt.

E1

5 MPH ZONE

E2

Bass Bay

E3

E4

MORGAN MARINE Ⓜ

Delaware Is.

E5

SNUG HARBOR SOUTH Ⓜ

E6

E7

F

N
W   E
S

SABBATH
DAY POINT

188

Excellent anchorages can be found in the numerous bays and coves in the vicinity of Huletts Landing. Depths in these areas average between 20 to 30 feet. Avoid dropping anchor in high-traffic areas, and remember to respect private property. Though less protected, several decent anchorages can be found along the west shore including Bass, Silver, and Van Buren Bays.

▮ Ashore

Lodging

Motels, resorts, cottages and houses are available in Huletts Landing and in the Sabbath Day Point and Silver Bay areas. In Huletts Landing, *Huletts-on-the-Lake* (518-499-1234) offers lakeside houses and cottages, golf, dockage for guests, and the "Casino" recreation center. They also offer live entertainment.

Near Silver Bay on the west side of the lake there are several options for lodging. *Northbrook Cottages* (518-543-6020) offers cottages, a private beach, and dockage for guests. Just to the north is *Carol's Cozy Cottages* (814-440-0679), providing cottages, dockage, and waterfront deck. In Bass

Gull Island. Photo by Scott Padeni.

Bay the ***Northern Lake George Resort*** (518-543-6528) is a full-service, 4-season resort offering villas, lodges, and motel rooms. They also provide an on-site restaurant and bar, dockage, private beach, and numerous other amenities. Scuba Diving charters and lessons are also available.

Silver Bay YMCA of the Adirondacks (518-543-8833) located in Silver Bay was first established in 1909 as the Silver Bay Association. Today, it is an expansive campus providing conference centers, leadership and team-building training, and spiritual programs.

Dining

Dining options in this section of the lake include ***Martucci's Restaurant*** 518-543-6528) in the Uncas Room of the ***Northern Lake George Resort*** in Silver Bay. Dockage is available to patrons.

Although not accessible by boat, the ***Silver Bay General Store*** (518-543-6441) is located on Route 9N, just north of Van Buren Bay, and sells sandwiches, groceries, gas, supplies, beer, beverages, camping supplies, and firewood.

Entertainment and Attractions

The northern end of Lake George is not known for its nightlife, shopping, and glitzy attractions; rather, this region of the lake is known for its spectacular views, relaxation, and spending time in and on the water.

Hiking, kayaking, snorkeling, scuba diving, water skiing, and fishing are the most common activities. Powerboats, kayaks and canoes are available for rent by the local marinas and often available at local resorts and cottages.

The only boat-accessible golf course on Lake George is available at Huletts Landing. Call in advance to make docking arrangements (518-499-1234). For the history buff, Fort Ticonderoga is only a short drive north.

View from Washington County Beach. Photo by Peggy Huckel

The Northern End: Hague, Ticonderoga, Glenburnie, and Vicinity

The northern end of Lake George is home to the communities of Hague, Glenburnie, and Ticonderoga. Far from the hustle and bustle of Lake George's south end, its north end is more laid back, trading arcades and mini golf for relaxation and spectacular views. Lake George's north end is also its outlet, where the waters of the lake cascade 220 feet down the La Chute Creek through the Town of Ticonderoga into Lake Champlain. Because of this drastic difference in elevation between the two lakes, the outlet is non-navigable, and the reason why Lake George is considered land-locked.

This section of the lake is also one of the most historically significant locations in the country. In 1755 during the French and Indian War, Fort Carillon (Ticonderoga) was built by the French to control the outlet of Lake George, which was a strategic water route into Lake Champlain. This fort also played a key role during the American Revolution. Years later, during the 19th century, Hague and Ticonderoga became industrial centers producing lumber, graphite, iron, and paper. Evidence of this military and industrial activity can be found today in the numerous shipwrecks resting on the lake bottom.

▌ Navigation

Some of the deepest waters of Lake George are found in this region of the lake, particularly off the vertical rock face of Anthony's Nose along the east shore, where depths reach 185 feet. The lake's widest point in this area is just over 2 miles from Hague across to Gull Bay on the east shore.

Navigation in this region of the lake is relatively straightforward with a modest number of shoals generally hugging both shorelines. Traveling north, several isolated shoals are encountered along the east shore. **Burnt Point Reef** is an isolated shoal located about 450 feet southwest of Burnt Point. Further north, keep your eyes open for **Gull Island** and associated shoals located about a quarter mile west of the entrance to Gull Bay. These shoals are marked by lighted can buoys "C2" and "C3." Beware of several other shoals along the east shore between Gull Bay and Anthony's Nose. Each are marked by unlighted cans or spars. Gull Bays and Dark Bays are designated as 5 mph zones.

LAKE GEORGE'S NORTHERN END

TICONDEROGA

6 M

5

See page 202

See page 204

Hearts Bay

A4

B BB

Weeds Bay

B2

B1

Rogers Rock
(Rogers Slide)

I 3

Mooring Field
Cooks Bay

B3

Anthony's Nose

Friends Pt.

B4

GLENBURNIE

Blair's Bay

Brown's Pt.

4

Waltonian Is.

2

C

HAGUE

1

B5

5 MPH ZONE

C1

See page 194

Dark Bay

See page 200

Wreck of the
John Jay

Gull Is.

C3

C2

Gull Bay

D2

0 mi.   1 mi.   2 mi.

192

N
W E
S

Scale of Miles

Lake George's Northern End map key

1. Ruah B&B
2. Northern Lake George Yacht Club
3. Rogers Rock Campground 🚹
4. Adirondack Camp
5. Mossy Point Boat Launch 🚹
6. Snug Harbor Marina

🚹 Inspection station Ⓜ Marina

On the approach north along the west shore stay clear of a large gravelly delta off Jenkins Point. About a mile north in Hague, an extensive shallow is also located at the mouth of Hague Brook and just off the Hague public beach and boat launch. This shallow delta extends about 450 feet offshore. Both the Jenkins and Hague Brook deltas are marked by can and spar buoys.

Three quarters of a mile north are the Waltonian Islands. Spar buoys mark random shoals that are found among these islands. The waters surrounding the Waltonian Islands are designated as a 5 mph zone. Be watchful for swimmers when navigating among these islands as they are a favorite among campers.

Beyond Friends Point, few hazards to navigation are found until you get beyond the bare stone face of Rogers Slide. At the entrance to Hearts Bay, lighted can buoy "B1" and spars identify a shoal extending 290 feet off Hawk-eye (Windmill) Point on the west shore. Several shoals are also located in the center of Hearts Bay, marked by unlighted cans and spars. Another isolated shoal at the end of Coates Point at the north entrance to Hearts Bay is marked by lighted can buoy "A4" and a spar. On the opposite side of the lake in Weeds Bay, several shoals are marked by unlighted cans and spars.

The remaining portion of the lake north of Black Point is extremely shallow with numerous shoals and other submerged hazards. To navigate this portion of the lake, follow the channel marked by green and red buoys, being sure to keep the red to port if traveling north. The south end of the channel is situated just off Black Point. From there, the channel winds its way north past Prisoners Island, continuing another two miles to a bedrock obstruction known as the Natural Stone Dam. This point marks the end of navigational aids on the lake.

A very narrow cut was blasted through the Natural Stone Dam in the 1800s allowing smaller vessels to pass. If unfamiliar with the waters, however, passing through this cut is not advisable as there is little room for error, and currents are often strong. Many a prop and lower unit have been claimed attempting this route. The lake beyond the natural stone dam is shallow and weedy, ending three quarters of a mile north at a dam where the lake water

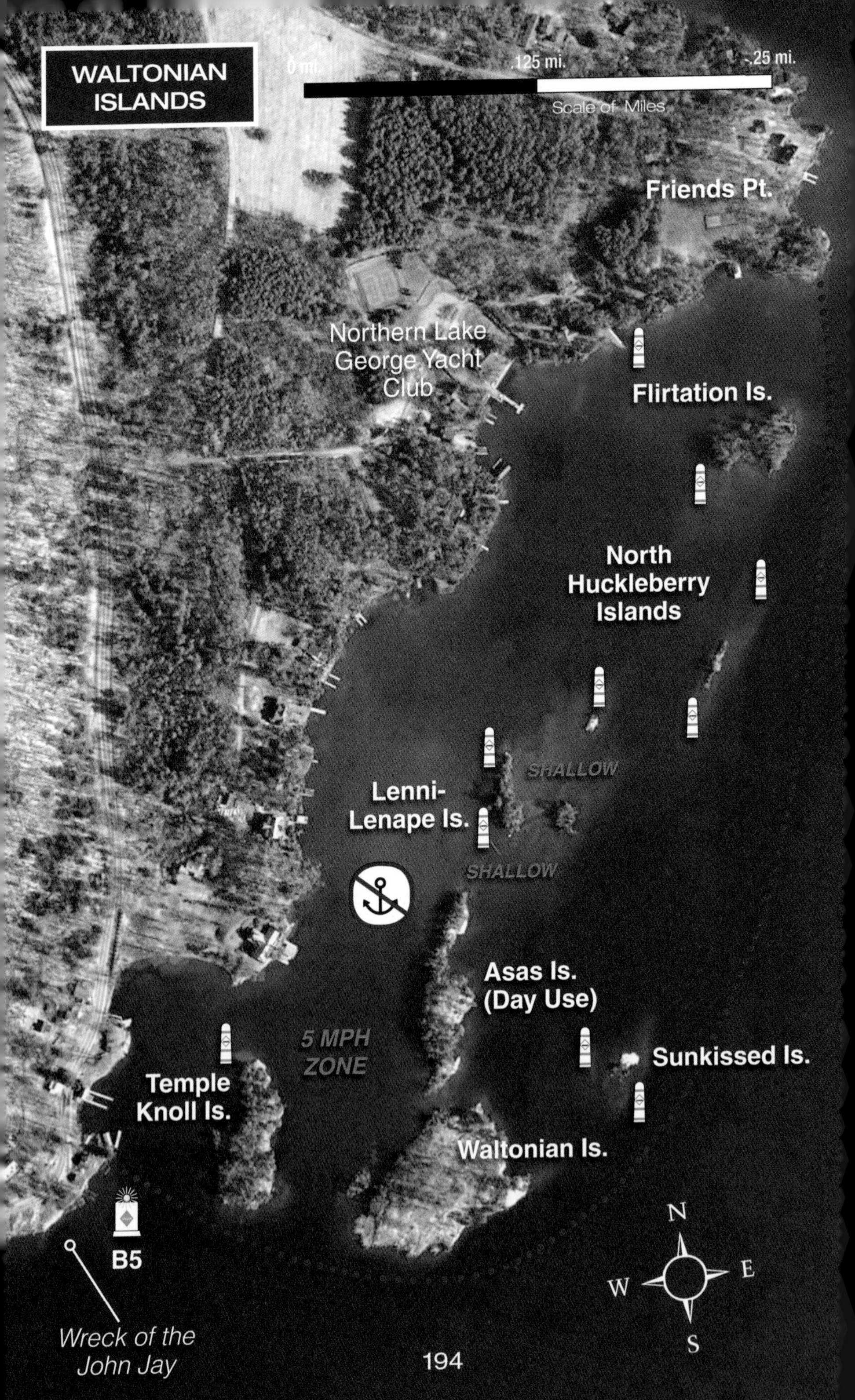

WALTONIAN ISLANDS

0 mi.   .125 mi.   .25 mi.
Scale of Miles

Friends Pt.

Northern Lake George Yacht Club

Flirtation Is.

North Huckleberry Islands

SHALLOW

Lenni-Lenape Is.

SHALLOW

Asas Is. (Day Use)

Sunkissed Is.

5 MPH ZONE

Temple Knoll Is.

Waltonian Is.

B5

N
W   E
S

Wreck of the John Jay

194

begins its 220 foot drop into Lake Champlain. Just before the dam is the Alexandria Avenue Bridge. Do not attempt to pass under the bridge as large unmarked rocks lie just below the surface.

The lake north of Mossy Point, beginning at channel markers "1" and "2," is designated as a 5 mph zone.

▌Marinas and Launches

Several launching facilities and two marinas are located in this region of the lake. In Hague, on the west shore, ***Dockside Landing Marina*** (518-543-8888) provides gas, transient docking, boat rentals, a ships store with marine and camping supplies, snacks and beverages, repair service, public restrooms, emergency towing and sells LGPC stickers. They do not have launching facilities.

Launching facilities and restrooms can be found just to the south at the ***Hague Town Park***. Launching cost is a $10 day-use fee that includes parking, short-term dockage, and use of their beach. Use care when launching or landing here, as depths in the vicinity of the town launch are shallow with a gravelly bottom, the result of sediments from nearby Hague Brook. Dredging of this delta is planned for the near future.

View looking east from the shore in Hague. Photo by Peggy Huckel

Launching facilities are also available just over three miles north at the NY State-owned *Rogers Rock Public Campground*. The launch facilities here are excellent with short-term dockage, restrooms, pump-out, beach, hot showers, picnic pavilion, and other amenities available. Cost to launch is a $6.00 day-use fee. **This is an official inspection staion.**

Three miles north on the east shore, another NY State-owned launch facility is also available. The *Mossy Point Boat Launch* is located two miles north of Ticonderoga on Black Point Road. This launch facility has ample short-term dockage, restrooms, pump-out facilities, and parking for over 100 vehicles. Launching at this facility is free. **This is an official inspection staion.**

Snug Harbor Marina (518-585-2628) is located on Black Point Road in Ticonderoga, just south of the Natural Stone Dam at the lake's north end. They are a full service marina with boat launching facilities, boat storage and winterization, transient dockage, boat rental, fuel, repairs, and public restrooms.

▌ Dockage, Mooring, and Anchoring

Short-term and/or transient dockage is available at the above-mentioned launch facilities and marinas. Dockage is also available with the island camping sites and day-use Asas Island, located at the Waltonian Islands in Hague.

Thirty public mooring buoys are available at Rogers Rock Campground for $15 per day, in addition to campsite fee. You can make your reservations up to nine months in advance, which is advisable, as sites and moorings go quickly. To reserve a mooring, you must first have a campsite reservation.

The plentiful coves and bays at the northern region of the lake provide ample choices for anchoring. Just remember to respect local residents and to not anchor closer than 200 feet from private property. One of my favorite anchorages is Gull Bay on the east side of the lake, which offers protection from most winds. Depths in the bay average around 20 feet. The lower half of Gull Bay is a designated 5 mph zone.

When making your approach, stay clear of Gull Island Shoals about a quarter mile west of the bay entrance.

Anchoring is also possible in the shallows north of Black Point outside the marked channel, though most of the bottom in this area consists of mud and grass. Other anchoring options include Heart and Weeds Bays with average depths of 20–30 feet.

Anchoring among the Waltonian Islands is prohibited. Remember that there is a 5 mph zone when navigating among the islands, and beware of shoals.

Rogers Rock. Photo by Scott Padeni.

The History Behind Rogers Rock

Rogers Rock has a colorful history behind its name. On March 13, 1758 during the French and Indian War, 180 British and American Provincial Rangers were attacked and nearly annihilated by the French at the "Second Battle on Snowshoes" fought at Bald Mountain at the north end of Lake George. The Rangers were under the command of Major Robert Rogers, an intrepid leader who developed unconventional tactics for fighting in the harsh environment of the Lake George and Lake Champlain valleys. Known as "Rogers 28 Rules of Ranging," his tactics remain in use today by the U.S. Army Rangers. Over 120 of Roger's men were lost in the engagement. Rogers survived, and became legendary as rumors spread that he escaped by sliding down the 500-foot east face of Bald Mountain. The rock face has since been known as Rogers Rock, or Rogers Slide.

▌Ashore

Lodging

● The *Hague Motel* (518-543-6631) is located on the lakeshore in Hague. The motel is adjacent to the Hague Town Park and boat launch and offers cabins or motel rooms, beach, kayaks, and canoes. Dockage is available at the adjacent public docks.

● *Trout House Village Resort* (518-543-6088) is also located in Hague on Lake Shore Drive just a short distance north of Hague Park. The original Trout House Hotel was one of the earliest hotels on the northern lake. Today, the Patchett family operates this expansive four-season resort and offers log cabins, cottages, and rooms. They also offer numerous amenities including dockage, a large beach, kayaks, rowboats, miniature golf, basketball, and other activities on-site.

● *Ruah B&B* (518-543-8816) is situated on Shore Drive overlooking Lake George and the Waltonian Islands. This elegant award-winning inn is over 100 years old and offers relaxation, gourmet breakfasts, and spectacular views of Lake George.

● *Rogers Rock Campground (and Waltonian Islands)* (518-585-6746) is located in the Town of Hague and is operated by the State of New York. The campground has 332 campsites. Amenities include 2 group camping areas; picnic area with tables, picnic pavilion rentals, fireplaces, flush toilets, hot showers, boat launch, mooring buoys, boat pump out facilities, large sand beach with lifeguards, and bathhouse. **This is an official inspection staion.**

Reservations can be made at: http://newyorkstateparks.reserveamerica.com/camping. Camping fees are $22 per night. Moorings are $15 per day. Ten campsites are located on the Waltonian Islands near Friends Point.

HAGUE DOCKS

Trout House Village Resort

Dockside Landing Marina

Uptown Store
Hague Firehouse
Restaurant

Hague Market

SHALLOW

Hague Town Beach

SHALLOW

Restrooms

SHALLOW

Hague Boat Launch

Hague Motel

SHALLOW

D

SHALLOW

D1

SHALLOW

N
W   E
S

0 ft.   500 ft.   1000 ft.

Scale of Feet

Dining

Three eateries are located along Graphite Mountain Road within a short walking distance of the Hague Town boat launch and docks.

- The *Hague Firehouse Restaurant* (518-543-6266) is located less than a 10-minute walk from the town docks, and serves American grill, bistro, and casual dining. They also have a take-out menu for boaters.

- A few doors down is the *Uptown Store* (518-543-6202) serving family style dining.

- Closest to the town docks is the *Hague Market* (518-543-6555), Closest to the town docks is the Hague Market (518-543-6555) which sells breakfast and lunch sandwiches, groceries, beer and ice. ATM available. 2nd floor gifts and boutique!

TICONDEROGA

TICONDEROGA

0 ft.   1000 ft.   2000 ft.   3000 ft.
Scale of Feet

N
W   E
S

Natural Stone Dam

End of navigational buoys on Lake George

5 mph zone

M

I

See page 204

Mossy Point Public Boat Launch

2   1

Mossy Pt.

4   3

SHALLOW

Howes Landing

6   5

SHALLOW

Prisoners Is.

Coates Pt.

8   7

8A

7A

A5

Black Pt.

A4

A3

202

Entertainment and Attractions

● One of the greatest attractions at the north end of Lake George is *Fort Ticonderoga* (518-585-2821). Fort Ticonderoga (Carillon) was built in 1755 by the French during the French and Indian War (1754–1763) and is arguably one of the most historic sites in North America. Reconstructed in the early 1900s, today its museum houses one of the country's largest French and Indian War and American Revolution collections. Although not accessible by boat from Lake George, Fort Ticonderoga is only 2 ½ miles from the Mossy Point boat launch in the Town of Ticonderoga.

● The *Adirondack Camp* (518-547-8261) is a traditional youth summer camp located on the south shore of Blairs Bay in the Town of Putnam. The camp has been operating for over 100 years. Campers enjoy traditional activities including sailing, fishing, boating, archery, hiking, white-water rafting, swimming, and more.

● *Northern Lake George Yacht Club* (518-543-6533) is located at Friends Point in Hague, and dates back to the late 1800s. One of the main missions of this club is the sponsorship of youth programs and regattas for kids between 3 and 16. They offer instruction in sailing, tennis, swimming, and life-saving.

● *Justy-Joe Charters and Guide Service* (518-798-0336), also based out of Hague, is available for guided fishing trips and lake charters.

Shopping is available upstairs above the *Hague Market* at the *Juniper ON 2 Boutique and Gift Shop*.

Several excellent **SCUBA diving** sites are in this portion of the lake. A favorite is at the base of Rogers Rock. The 500-foot granite face of Rogers Rock continues another 100 feet below the surface. The vertical granite wall makes for an almost surreal dive in visibilities that can exceed 60 feet. Another excellent dive site in this region of the lake is the wreck of the Steamboat *John Jay*, which sank on July 29, 1856 near the Waltonian Islands. The wreck is located just off shore in 10 feet of water, south of Temple Knoll Island and lighted can buoy "B5." Wreckage continues into deeper water. The wreck is shallow enough for snorkeling.

MOSSY POINT AND
NATURAL STONE DAM

5 mph zone

Natural
Stone Dam

A

Snug Harbor
Marina

M

N
W E
S

SHALLOW

5 mph zone

5 mph zone

I

Public Boat
Launch

Mossy Pt.

204

0 mi.   .125 mi   .25

Scale of Miles

Directories and Appendices

Lake George Park Commission
Boat Registration Vendors by Location • 1

Name	Phone (518 Area Code)	Address	Location
Lake George Chamber of Commerce	668-5755	Fort George Rd & Rte. 9	Lake George 12845
Hall's Boat Corporation	668-5437	East Side of Village	Lake George 12845
Beach Rd Bait & Tackle	668-4040	Canada St	Lake George 12845
Lake George Mini-Chopper	668-2337	49 Amherst St	Lake George 12845
Adirondack Marine	668-2658	3226 Lakeshore Dri	Lake George 12845
Warren County Clerk	761-6516	W.C. Municipal Center, 1340 Rte. 9	Lake George 12845
Boats By George	793-5452	18 State Rte 149	Lake George 12845
Fish 307.com	798-9203	1571 State Rte 9	Lake George 12845
Sportline Power Products	792-4655	38 East Quaker Rd	Queensbury 12804
Town of Queensbury	761-8234	742 Bay Rd	Queensbury 12804
Dunham's Bay Boat & Beach Club	656-9827	18 Dunham's Bay Rd	Queensbury 12804
Castaway Marina	656-3636	2546 Route 9L	Queensbury 12845
Boats By George On The Lake	656-9353	291 Cleverdale Rd	Cleverdale 12820
Fischer's Marina	656-9981	1215 Pilot Knob Rd	Pilot Knob 12844
Pilot Knob Marina	656-9211	1881 Pilot Knob Rd	Pilot Knob 12844
Outdoorsman Sport Shop	668-3910	3619 Lake Shore Dr	Diamond Point 12824
Blue Lagoon Resort	668-4867	3670 Lake Shore Drive	Diamond Point 12845
Gilchrist Marina	668-2028	3686 Lake Shore Dr	Diamond Point 12824
Yankee Boating Center	668-2862	3910 Lake Shore Dr (9N)	Diamond Point 12824
Beckley's Boats	668-2651	3950 Lake Shore Dr (9N)	Diamond Point 12824

Lake George Park Commission
Boat Registration Vendors by Location • 2

Name	Phone (518 Area Code)	Address	Location
Bay View Marina	644-9633	4762 Lake Shore Dr (9N)	Bolton Landing 12814
Chic's Marina	644-2170	4782 Lake Shore Dr (9N)	Bolton Landing 12814
Lake George Camping Equipment	644-9941	North Main St	Bolton Landing 12814
NOROWAL Marina	644-3741	21 Sagamore Rd	Bolton Landing 12814
F.R. Smith & Son's, Inc.	644-5181	36 Sagamore Rd	Bolton Landing 12814
Silver Bay General Store	543-6441	8417 Lake Shore Dr	Silver Bay 12874
Hague Market	543-6555	Route 8 (9844 Graphite Mountain Rd)	Hague 12836
Dockside Landing Marina	543-8888	930 Lake Shore Dr, Route 9N	Hague 12836
Tony's Ti Sports	585-6364	9N and Route 22	Ticonderoga 12883
Town of Ticonderoga	585-6677	132 Montcalm St	Ticonderoga 12883
Snug Harbor Marina	585-2628	Black Point Rd (36 Lake George Ave)	Ticonderoga 12883
Huletts Landing Marina	499-0801	East Shore	Huletts Landing 12841
Ti Food Mart	585-7527	66 Montcalm St	Ticonderoga 12883

MANDATORY INSPECTION STATIONS

Town	Location
Lake George	Lake George Inspection Station, Transfer Road
Bolton Landing	Norowal Marina, 21 Sagamore Road
Hague	Rogers Rock Campground, 9894 Lakeshore Drive
Ticonderoga	Mossy Point Public Boat Launch, Black Point Road
Queensbury	Dunham's Bay Marina, 2036 Bay Road
Huletts Landing	Huletts Landing Marina, 6068 Lakeside Way

Lake George Area Attractions

Amusement Parks, Adventure and Watersports

Adirondack Adventures Rafting	North River	(877) 963-7238
Adirondack Balloon Flights	Glens Falls	(518) 793-6342
Adirondack Extreme Adventures	Bolton Landing	(518) 494-7200
Adirondack Rafting Company	Indian Lake	(800) 510-7238
Adventure Racing Family Center	1079 State Route 9, Queensbury	(518) 798-7860
Dr. Morbid's Haunted House of Wax	115 Canada St., LG Village	(518) 668-3077
The Fun Spot	1035 State Route 9, Queensbury	(518) 792-8989
Hillbilly Fun Park	Route 149, Fort Ann	(518) 792-5239
House of Frankenstein Wax Museum	Canada St., LG Village	(518) 668-3377
Hudson River Rafting Company	North Creek	(800) 888-7238
Lake George Batting Cages	State Route 9, Lake George	(518) 668-3223
Magic Castle Rides & Indoor Golf	275 Canada St., LG Village	(518) 668-3777
Magic Forest	State Route 9, Lake George	(518) 668-2448
North Country Heliflite	Harris Airport–83K 10915 St Rt 149, Ft. Ann, NY	(518) 361-1380
Saddle Up Stables	3513 Lake Shore Drive, Lake George	(518) 668-4801
Six Flags Great Escape	1172 State Route 9, Queensbury	(518) 792-3500
Tubby Tubes Company (tubing, rafting)	Lake Luzerne	(518) 696-7222
Waterslide World	2136 State Route 9, Lake George	(518) 668-4407
Wild Waters Outdoor Center	Route 28, Warrensburg	(518) 494-4984

Beaches

Washington County Beach	Huletts Landing	(518) 746-2440
Usher's Park Beach	State Route 9L, Lake George	(518) 668-0034
Million Dollar Beach	Beach Road, LG Village	(518) 668-3352
Shepard's Park Beach	Canada Street, LG Village	(518) 644-9366
Rogers Memorial Park Beach	Bolton Landing	(518) 644-3831
Veteran's Memorial Park Beach	Bolton Landing	(518) 644-3831
Robert E. Henry Memorial Park	Hague	(518) 543-6161
Black Point Beach	Ticonderoga	(518) 585-7139

Bowling

Sparetime Family Fun Center	State Route 9, Lake George	(518) 668-5741

Boat , Kayak, and Stand Up Paddleboard Rentals

Boats by George and Patty's Water Sports Boutique	Cleverdale	(518) 656-9353
Captain Bob's Boat Rental	Bolton Landing	(518) 644-5921
Chic's Marina	Bolton Landing	(518) 644-2170
Dockside Landing Marina	Hague	(518) 543-8888
Dunham's Bay Boat Co.	Dunhams Bay Road, Lake George	(518) 656-9244
Fischer's Marina	Kattskill Bay	(518) 656-9981
F.R. Smith & Sons Marina	Bolton Landing	(518) 644-5181
Gilchrist Marina	Diamond Point	(518) 668-2028
Kayak Lake George	LG Village	(518) 302-6005
Lake George Camping Equipment & Marina	Bolton Landing	(518) 644-9941
Lake George Boat Rentals	LG Village	(518) 685-5331
Lake George Kayak Company	Bolton Landing	(518) 644-9366
Snug Harbor South Boat Rentals	Silver Bay	(518) 543-8866
U-Drive Boat Rentals	LG Village	518-668-4644
Waters Edge Marina	3910 Lake Shore Drive, Diamond Point	(518) 644-2511
Yankee Boating Center (boat rentals)	3578 Lake Shore Drive, Lake George	(518) 668-2862

Churches (by location)

Assembly of God	Bolton Landing	(518) 644-2412
Church of Saint Sacrament Episcopal	Bolton Landing	(518) 644-9613
Emmanuel United Methodist	Bolton Landing	(518) 644-9962
First Baptist Church	Bolton Landing	(518) 644-9103
Blessed Sacrament Church	Bolton Landing	(518) 644-3861
Methodist Church Emmanuel United	Bolton Landing	(518) 644-9962
Diamond Point Community Church	Diamond Point	(518) 668-2722
Lakeside Regional Church,	Hague	(518) 543-4594

Church of the Blessed Sacrament	Hague	(518) 543-8828
Hague Baptist Church	Hague	(518) 543-8899
Chapel of the Assumption	Kattskill Bay	(518) 656-9034
Caldwell Presbyterian Church	LG Village	(518) 668-2613
Redeemer Reformed Presbyterian Church	LG Village	(518) 761-0874
Sacred Heart Church	LG Village	(518) 668-2046
St. James Episcopal Church	LG Village	(518) 668-2001
St. Mary's	Ticonderoga	(518) 585-7144

Excursion and Dinner Boats

Lake George Steamboat Company	Beach Road, LG Village	(518) 668-2015
Shoreline Cruises	2 Kurosaka Lane, LG Village	(518) 668-4644
The *Morgan*, Sagamore Resort	Bolton Landing	(518) 644-9400

Fishing Charters

C Monster Sport Fishing	Bolton Landing	(518) 791-9200
E & R Sport Fishing Charters	Lake George	(800) 336-6987
Highliner Charter Fishing	3926 Lake Shore Drive, Diamond Point	(518) 885-3838
Hooker Charters	Flamingo Resort, Diamond Point	(518) 668-5052
Indian Pipes Chartered Cruises	Bolton Landing	(845) 772-1177
Jeff's Lake George Fishing Charters	Bolton Landing	(518) 644-3312
Justy-Joe's Fishing Charters	Hague	(877) 249-7472
Lockhart Guide Service	Kattskill Bay	(518) 812-0203
Mickey Finn Fly Fishing	Kattskill Bay	(518) 423-6074
Risky Business Charter Fishing	Bolton Landing	(518) 623-9582
Rod Bender Charters	Diamond Point	(518) 668-5657

Golf and Mini Golf

Around the World Golf	Beach Road, LG Village	(518) 668-2531
Country Meadows Golf	State Route 149, Fort Ann	(518) 792-5927
Goony Golf	127 Canada Street, LG Village	(518) 668-2589

Huletts Landing Golf Course	Huletts Landing	(518) 499-1234
Lumberjack Pass Mini Golf	State Route 9 & 149, Lake George	(518) 793-7141
Pirates Cove Mini Golf	215 State Route 9, Lake George	(518) 668-0493
Putts & Prizes	Beach Road, Lake George	(518) 668-9500
Queensbury Country Club	State Route 149, Lake George	(518) 793-3711
Sagamore Resort	Bolton Landing	(518) 644-9400
Ticonderoga Country Club	Ticonderoga	(518) 585-2801
Top of the World Golf Course	Lake George	(518) 668-3000

Libraries

Bolton Free Library	Main St., Bolton Landing	(518) 644-2233
Caldwell-Lake George Library	340 Canada St, LG Village	(518) 668-2528
Diamond Point Community Library	Lake Shore Dr., Diamond Point	(518) 668-2528

Parasailing

Parasail Adventures	LG Village	(607) 272-7245
Parasail Joe's	LG Village	(518) 668-4013
Para-sail Sunsports Unlimited	Chic's Marina, Bolton Landing	(518) 644-3470

Spas

The Sagamore Resort	Bolton Landing	(518) 644-9400

Scuba Diving

Halfmoon Marine Services	Bolton Landing	(518) 357-3234
Rich Morin's Pro Scuba Center	20 Warren Street, Glens Falls	(518) 761-0533
Seguin's Scuba Center	1629 Central Avenue, Albany	(518) 456-8146

Theatre, Museums, History and the Arts

Adirondack Museum	Blue Mountain Lake	(518) 352-7311
Bolton Historical Society Museum	Main St., Bolton Landing	(518) 644-9960
Bolton Gallery & Art Center	Lakeshore Drive, Bolton Landing	(518) 644-9480
Clifton West Museum	Hague Community Center	(518) 543-6161

Courthouse Gallery	Old County Courthouse, LG Village	(518) 668-2616
Fort Ticonderoga	Ticonderoga, NY	(518) 585-2821
Fort William Henry Museum	48 Canada Street, LG Village	(800) 234-0267
Lake George Battlefield Park	LG Village	(518) 668-3352
Lake George Historical Association Museum	Old County Courthouse LG Village	(518) 668-5044
Lake George Dinner Theater	State Route 9, Holiday Inn, LG Village	(518) 793-6342
Marcella Sembrich Opera Museum	Bolton Landing	(518) 644-2431
Terrace Room Dinner Theatre	384 Canada St., LG Village	(518) 668-5401
Submerged Heritage Preserve	Lake George	(518) 897-1200
Sweet Pea Farm Perennials & Art Gallery	Bolton Landing	(518) 644-3020

Train, Trolley, and Carriage Rides

Lake George Carriage Rides	Lake George Village	(518) 696-5836
Lake George Village Trolley	LG Village/Bolton Landing	(518) 792-1085
Upper Hudson River Railroad	North Creek	(518) 251-5842

Wine Tasting & Breweries

Adirondack Winery & Tasting Room	285 Canada St., LG Village	(518) 668-9463
Adirondack Pub & Brewery	33 Canada St, LG Village	(518) 668-0002
Coopers Cave Ale Company	2 Sagamore Street, Glens Falls	(518) 792-0007

Lake George Marinas • 1

MARINA	Transient Dockage	Launch	Fuel	Pumpout
Adirondack Marina (518) 668-2658	NO	NO	NO	NO
Bayview Marina (518)644-9633)	YES	NO	NO	NO
Beckley's Boats (518) 668-2651	NO	YES	YES	NO
Boardwalk Restaurant and Marina (518) 668-4828	YES	NO	YES	YES
Boats by George (518) 656-9353 (See ad on page 91)	NO	YES	YES	YES
Bolton Landing Marina (518) 644-3474	NO	NO	YES	YES
Castaway Marina (518) 656-3636 (See ad on page 112)	NO	YES	YES	YES
Chics Marina (518) 644-2170	NO	NO	YES	NO
Dockside Landing Marina (518) 543-8888 (See ad on page 196)	YES	NO	YES	NO
Dunham's Bay Boat Company (518) 656-9244	NO	NO	YES	YES
Dunham's Bay Marina (518) 744-2627	YES	YES	NO	NO
Fischer's Marina (518) 656-9981 (See ad on page 121)	YES	YES	YES	YES

Repairs	Supplies	Showers/ Restrooms	Boat Regis- trations	Tow	Boat Rental
YES	NO	NO	YES	NO	NO
YES	NO	YES	YES	NO	NO
YES	NO	NO	YES	NO	NO
NO	YES	RESTROOMS	NO	NO	NO
YES	MARINE STORE AND BAIT	RESTROOMS & SHOWERS	YES	NO	NO
NO	NO	MEMBERS ONLY	NO	NO	NO
YES	MARINE STORE	RESTROOMS	YES	NO	NO
YES	MARINE STORE	RESTROOMS	YES	NO	YES
YES	GROCERIES	RESTROOMS	YES	YES	YES
YES	MARINE STORE	RESTROOMS	YES	YES	YES
NO	NO	RESTROOMS	NO	NO	NO
YES	GROCERIES AND BAIT	RESTROOMS	YES	YES	YES

Lake George Marinas • 2

MARINA	Transient Dockage	Launch	Fuel	Pumpout
F. R. Smith & Sons (518) 644-5181	YES	NO	YES	NO
Gilchrist Marina (518) 668-5848	YES	YES	NO	NO
Halls Boat Corp. (518) 668-5437	YES	NO	YES	YES
Harris Bay Yacht Club (518) 656-9028 (See ad on page 120)	NO	NO	YES	YES
Huletts Landing Marina (518) 499-0801 (518) 499-9949	YES	YES	YES	NO
Lake George Camping Co. and Marina (518) 644-9941	YES	YES	YES	NO
Lake George Boat Company (518) 656-9203	NO	YES	YES	YES
Morgan Marine (518) 543-6666	NO	NO	YES	NO
Norowal Marina (518) 644-3741	YES	YES	YES	YES
Pilot Knob Marina (518) 656-9211	NO	NO	YES	NO

Repairs	Supplies	Showers/ Restrooms	Boat Regis- trations	Tow	Boat Rental
YES	MARINE STORE	RESTROOMS	YES	YES	YES
YES	GROCERIES AND BAIT	RESTROOMS	YES	NO	YES
YES	NO	RESTROOMS	YES	YES	NO
YES	MARINE STORE	RESTROOMS AND SHOWERS	NO	YES	NO
NO	MARINE STORE, BAIT GROCERIES	RESTROOMS	YES	YES	CANOES & KAYAKS
YES	NO	NO	YES	YES (U.S. TOW)	YES
YES	NO	NO	NO	YES	NO
YES	NO	RESTROOMS	YES	YES	NO
YES	YES	RESTROOMS, SHOWERS, LAUNDRY	YES	NO	NO
YES	MARINE STORE	RESTROOMS	YES	NO	NO

Lake George Marinas • 3

MARINA	Transient Dockage	Launch	Fuel	Pumpout
Performance Marine (518) 644-3080	NO	NO	NO	NO
Shoreline Marina & Restaurant (518) 668-4644 (See ad on page 97)	NO	NO	NO	NO
Snug Harbor Marina (518) 585-2628	YES	NO	YES	NO
Snug Harbor South (518) 543-8866	NO	NO	YES	NO
Waters Edge Marina (518) 644-2511	NO	NO	YES	NO
Yankee Marine Center (518) 668-5696	NO	YES	YES	YES (LIMITED)

Public Boat Facilities

FACILITY				
DEC Mossy Point Boat Launch	NO	YES	NO	YES
DEC Northwest Bay Boat Launch (Car top only)	NO	YES	NO	NO
DEC Million Dollar Beach Boat Launch	NO	YES	NO	NO
DEC Rogers Rock Campground	NO	YES	NO	NO
Town of Hague Boat Launch	NO	YES	NO	NO

Repairs	Supplies	Showers/ Restrooms	Boat Regis- trations	Tow	Boat Rental
YES	NO	YES	NO	YES	NO
NO	NO	NO	NO	NO	YES
YES	MARINE STORE, BAIT GROCERIES	RESTROOMS	YES	NO	YES
NO	MARINE STORE, BAIT GROCERIES	RESTROOMS	YES	NO	YES
NO	GROCERIES AND BAIT	RESTROOMS	NO	NO	YES
YES	YES	RESTROOMS	YES	NO	YES

NO	NO	RESTROOMS	NO	NO	NO
NO	NO	NO	NO	NO	NO
NO	NO	RESTROOMS	NO	NO	NO
NO	NO	RESTROOMS	NO	NO	NO
NO	NO	RESTROOMS	NO	NO	NO

AIDS TO NAVIGATION (ATON) SYMBOL KEY

  CAN BUOYS are cylindrical in shape, and can be used for regulatory markers, to mark the port, or left hand side of a channel, or occasionally for mooring buoys (though most mooring buoys are spherical). Can buoys may also be lighted.

  NUN BUOYS are conical in shape, used to mark the starboard, or right side of a channel. Nun buoys may also be lighted.

  SPAR BUOYS are slender buoys that are cylindrical to indicate speed zones, or tapered with a rounded top for danger zones. They are generally smaller than cans and nuns, and can be used in place of regulatory or channel markers. The color of the spar buoy determines its function. Spar buoys are not lighted.

   CHANNEL MARKERS are used when safe passage through a particular area can only be accomplished by following a specific route. Red and Green buoys marking the channel are often placed in pairs, though they may also be staggered due to existing conditions. When navigating a channel, red, even numbered nun buoys will mark the starboard (right) side of the channel when proceeding toward the head of navigation (returning), or in the case of Lake George, to the south. Green, odd numbered buoys, will mark the port (left) side of the channel. When proceeding through a channel, favor the right side of the channel, particularly in the presence of oncoming traffic. Do not pass too closely to channel markers, however, as their position may not be precise due to drift or current. Safe anchorage areas are marked on the maps with an anchor symbol.

Lighting of buoys is based on the buoy's function. Channel markers are lighted green or red, with white lights used on regulatory markers and mooring buoys. White lights on mooring buoys are steady light, so as not to be confused with regulatory buoys. Flashing lights are found on regulatory and/or channel markers. Quick flashing white lights (>50 flashes per minute) are typically used for buoys marking dangerous shoals or other hazards. Red and green channel lights may be solid or flashing.

Regulatory markers are buoys that mark local hazards to navigation, or information on rules or regulations relating to a specific area. These markers consist of white cans and/or spars with orange symbols. There are four types regulatory buoys used on Lake George.

Danger

A **Diamond** shape indicates **Danger** This marker may indicate a shoal, rock, log, wreck or other hazard to navigation. This marker may be alone indicating an isolated hazard, or it may be grouped with other danger buoys or spars indicating a large obstruction. NEVER pass between grouped hazard markers. Also, never pass between a hazard buoy and the shore, if the marker is located near shore. As with any navigation buoy, its location may not be precise, so give it a wide berth.

Exclusion

A diamond shape with a cross indicates a vessel exclusion area. Quite frequently, these exclusion areas indicate swimming areas, close proximity to dams, or any other area where there is a danger to the vessel's crew, or others in the vicinity.

Control

An orange circle indicates **Regulation** or **Control** markers. Common examples are no wake zones, or speed zones where the speed limit is marked within the circle. Failure to comply with regulatory markers is illegal and can result in a fine.

Information

Informational markers are buoys with a square symbol, and offer directions, distances, or other boater information. These buoys have no navigational significance.

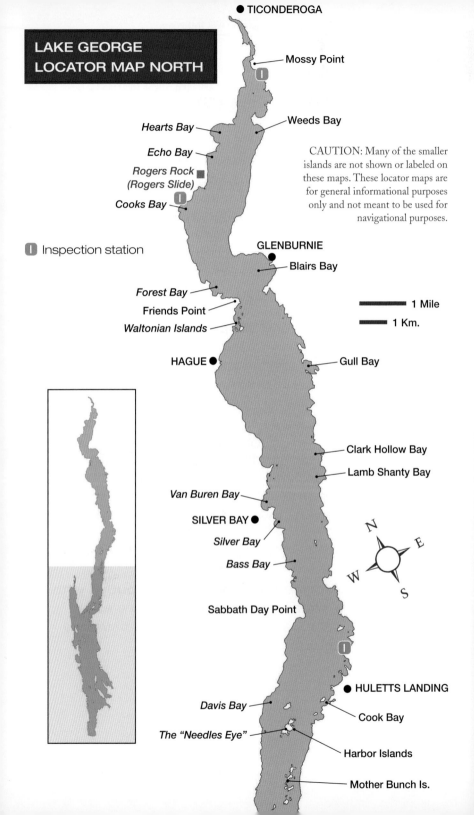

LAKE GEORGE LOCATOR MAP NORTH

● TICONDEROGA

Mossy Point

Weeds Bay

Hearts Bay

Echo Bay

Rogers Rock (Rogers Slide)

Cooks Bay

CAUTION: Many of the smaller islands are not shown or labeled on these maps. These locator maps are for general informational purposes only and not meant to be used for navigational purposes.

GLENBURNIE ●
Blairs Bay

I Inspection station

Forest Bay

Friends Point

Waltonian Islands

1 Mile

1 Km.

HAGUE ●
Gull Bay

Clark Hollow Bay

Lamb Shanty Bay

Van Buren Bay

SILVER BAY ●

Silver Bay

Bass Bay

N
E
W
S

Sabbath Day Point

● **HULETTS LANDING**

Davis Bay
Cook Bay

The "Needles Eye"

Harbor Islands

Mother Bunch Is.

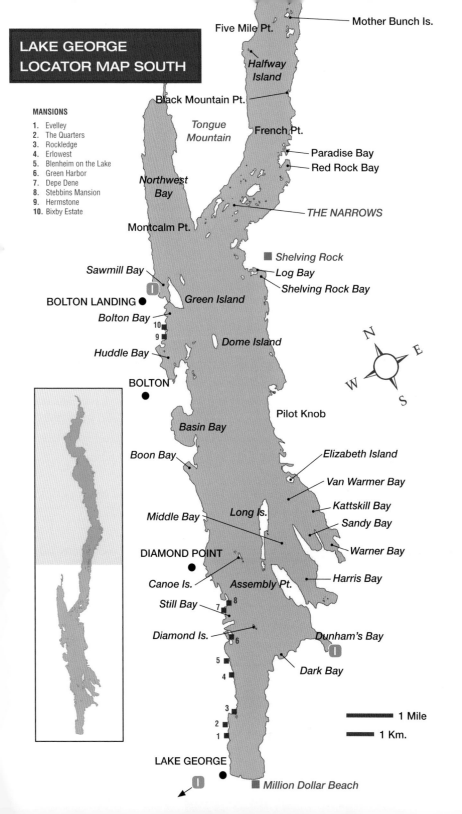

LAKE GEORGE LOCATOR MAP SOUTH

MANSIONS
1. Evelley
2. The Quarters
3. Rockledge
4. Erlowest
5. Blenheim on the Lake
6. Green Harbor
7. Depe Dene
8. Stebbins Mansion
9. Hermstone
10. Bixby Estate

Mother Bunch Is.
Five Mile Pt.
Halfway Island
Black Mountain Pt.
Tongue Mountain
French Pt.
Paradise Bay
Red Rock Bay
Northwest Bay
THE NARROWS
Montcalm Pt.
Shelving Rock
Sawmill Bay
Log Bay
Shelving Rock Bay
BOLTON LANDING
Green Island
Bolton Bay
Huddle Bay
Dome Island
BOLTON
Pilot Knob
Basin Bay
Boon Bay
Elizabeth Island
Van Warmer Bay
Middle Bay
Long Is.
Kattskill Bay
Sandy Bay
Warner Bay
DIAMOND POINT
Canoe Is.
Assembly Pt.
Harris Bay
Still Bay
Diamond Is.
Dunham's Bay
Dark Bay
LAKE GEORGE
Million Dollar Beach

N E W S

1 Mile
1 Km.

About the Authors

Scott A. Padeni is a professional mariner and published author with over 30 years of experience both above and below the waters of Lake George. During his career he has served as captain on numerous passenger vessels including Shoreline Cruise's 85' excursion vessel *Horicon*, as Engineer on the 115' *Adirondac*, and as Engineer for the Sagamore Hotel's 72'  *Morgan*. He has also served as a maritime instructor for The Nautical School, teaching USCG OUPV Captain and Master courses.

A veteran Nuclear Machinist Mate in the US Navy, Captain Padeni holds numerous maritime licenses and certifications, including a USCG Master License (100-gross tons near coastal with sail and tow endorsements); USCG instructor certifications; and certifications in CPR and First Aid for the Rescue Worker. He also holds American Sailing Association certifications including Basic Keelboat; Coastal Cruising; Bareboat, and Coastal Navigation.

With a bachelor's degree in history and archaeology, Scott has conducted numerous studies along the lakeshore and bellows its waters since 1995, documenting many Lake George shipwrecks and other archaeological sites. He has been diving the waters of Lake George since 1986, and holds nitrox and advanced diver certifications.

Captain Padeni presently resides in Dunedin, Florida and serves as Lead Captain and Engineer for the 120' dinner vessel *Starlite Sapphire*.

Peggy Huckel grew up on a lake, and learned to sail through a community sailing program at Maine Maritime Academy in Castine, Maine. She has lived in the Lake George area for nearly three decades. Holding a degree in American Studies from Skidmore College, a research and library science career complements her leisure-time activities in historical maritime reenacting, volunteering aboard several historical replica ships, serving as crew on  the gunboat *General Arnold* and the Mabee Farm bateaux, and as a board member of ASMA — the Age of Sail Maritime Alliance.

Adirondack Prints, Books, and Photography Workshops by Carl Heilman II

Carl Heilman II is an internationally published photographer and author who has been photographing the Adirondacks since the mid 1970's.His photographs capture the grandeur, as well as the spiritual connection he has to these special locations. His credits include Adirondack Life, the Conservationist, National Geographic Explorer, Outdoor Photographer, Shutterbug, the New York Times, coffee table books, and how-to books that are sold throughout the world. His Landscape Photography Field Guide and other techniques books offer creative photo tips from Carl's 4 decades of experience with a camera.

Carl enjoys working with people in his varied one day and multi-day photography workshops and tours. These are scheduled around the Adirondack Park, Acadia National Park, and other dramatic landscapes around the country. Please contact him to schedule unique, custom private tours, workshops, helicopter tours, and Photoshop instruction.

Look for Carl's 'mini' coffee table books, Lake George, and The Adirondacks (Rizzoli), and his photo techniques books in area stores, as well as his Lake George and Adirondacks wall calendars, panoramic puzzles, and posters. His hand signed and Special Edition fine art prints can be found in art collections around the world. Choose prints from image galleries on his website, or contact him with any special requests from his diverse collection of images from Lake George, the Adirondacks, New York state, the Maine coast, and other special locations around the country. He prints in color and black and white.

Information on Carl's workshops, tours, fine art prints, calendars, books, and puzzles is online at http://www.carlheilman.com On Facebook: https://www.facebook.com/NaturePhotographyWorkshops

Carl on First Peak in the Tongue Mtn. Range, photo by by Dr. William Brown.

Carl's books, calendars, puzzles, and custom prints can be purchased online and in stores throughout the Lake George area

223

NOTES